T0340915

The Secret People: Parish Pump Witchcraft, Wise-Women and Cunning Ways

The Secret People:
Parish Pump
Witchcraft,
Wise-Women and
Cunning Ways

Mélusine Draco

MOON
BOOKS

Winchester, UK
Washington, USA

First published by Moon Books, 2016
Moon Books is an imprint of John Hunt Publishing Ltd., Laurel House, Station Approach,
Alresford, Hants, SO24 9JH, UK
office1@jhpbooks.net
www.johnhuntpublishing.com
www.moon-books.net

For distributor details and how to order please visit the 'Ordering' section on our website.

ISBN: 978 1 78535 444 1
Library of Congress Control Number: 2016936942

A CIP catalogue record for this book is available from the British Library.

Design: Stuart Davies

Printed and bound by CPI Group (UK) Ltd, Croydon, CR0 4YY, UK

We operate a distinctive and ethical publishing philosophy in all
areas of our business, from our global network of authors to
production and worldwide distribution.

CONTENTS

Dedicated to the memory of my Father
who taught me to walk softly in the Wild Wood

About the Author

Mélusine Draco's highly individualistic teaching methods and writing draw on historical sources supported by academic texts and current archaeological findings; endorsing the view that magic is an amalgam of science and art, and that magic is the outer route to the inner Mysteries. Author of several titles currently published with John Hunt Publishing including the best-selling six-part Traditional Witchcraft series; two titles on power animals – *Aubry's Dog* and *Black Horse, White Horse*; *By Spellbook & Candle: Cursing, Hexing, Bottling and Binding*; *The Dictionary of Magic & Mystery* published by Moon Books; *Magic Crystals Sacred Stones* and *The Atum-Re Revival* published by Axis Mundi Books, she is also Principal of Coven of the Scales and the Temple of Khem.

Website: http://www.covenofthescales.com

Website: http://www.templeofkhem.com

Blog: http://melusinedracoattempleofkhem.blogspot.com/

Facebook:

https://www.facebook.com/Melusine-Draco-486677478165958

Facebook: http://www.facebook.com/TradBritOldCraft

Facebook: http:// www.facebook.com/TempleofKhem

Facebook: http://www.facebook.com/TempleHouseArchive

Introduction: Who am I?

Much of what passes for 'witchcraft' today was everyday knowledge to our forebears, especially those who lived and worked in the countryside. Here were to be found practical household hints, remedies and family recipes that had been handed down from generation to generation, some still existing in the form of treasured journals and notebooks. There is, however, nothing fanciful or far-fetched about this information – in fact, *The Secret People* is a remembrance of times past and a preservation of 'parish-pump witchcraft, wise woman and cunning ways' adapted for use in the 21st century. It may also go a long way in helping those present generation pagans in search of an identity and answer the questions: Who am I? What am I?

Most pagans now realise that the majority of Victorian compilations on superstitions are filled with protective charms against witchcraft, or warnings about the unlucky associations or omens attached to certain flora and fauna. For the genuine witch, no plant or animal is considered 'unlucky' since each has its own propensities that make it an integral part of Craft-lore. Because of the part certain plants played in healing, many were labelled evil or unlucky merely on account of them being part of the local 'wise woman's' stock in trade.

In both a historical and a social context, the wise woman was an important member of the community. A R Myers (*England in the Late Middle Ages*) recorded that when peasants fell ill, they relied chiefly on these local women, wise in the lore of herbs and other traditional remedies. Eric Maple (*Man, Myth & Magic*) also pointed out that what is not generally admitted is that in her heyday, the rural wise woman was doctor, veterinary surgeon and detective, called out to cure illness, administer to livestock and locate missing belongings in return for a 'gift' to supplement her meagre lifestyle.

1

Cunning folk were often travelling practitioners of domestic plant medicine, folk magic, and divination from medieval times up until the mid 20th century when the practice was slowly absorbed by the newly emerging neo-paganism. Like the European Romany, the basic belief of many cunning folk was generally Christianity and it was unusual for a cunning man or woman to actually be accused of witchcraft. The word 'cunning' means 'knowledge' or 'skilful' and was widely used in various contexts in Middle English from the 14th century onwards. Often a grandmother fondly remembered for reading the tea leaves and using plants from the garden to soothe childhood cuts and grazes, was keeping alive the traditions of the cunning folk without realising it.

According to Steve Roud in *The Penguin Guide to Superstitions of Britain and Ireland*:

> Cunning men and women were a regular feature of village and small town life for centuries...the majority of the populace would be well aware of who claimed powers in what context, and would could be paid for occult assistance, when necessary... The standard fare for the average cunning man or woman would also include fortune-telling, by various means, the location of lost or stolen property, love magic, the identification of spells cast upon the client...and measures to counter them, and magical healing techniques...

Margaret Murray (*The God of the Witches*) wrote that the contemporary idea of the witch is founded entirely in the records of the 16th and 18th centuries, when the Church was 'still hell-bent on eradicating the last vestiges of paganism'. This action was reinforced by support from the emerging medical profession, which viewed 'parish-pump' witchcraft as its most dangerous rival. As a result, local witches and wise women were often forced to administer their skills in secret for fear of reprisal. Over the years, however, many of the cures and charms were 'updated' to exclude any traditional practices and to keep superstitions in line with Church teaching, with many old charms now being addressed to saints since the Devil was associated with native customs.

Today, most 'natural' witches are what would have been referred to as the 'parish-pump' variety in that they are generally solitary and do not belong to an initiatory tradition or lineage. This is not a derogatory term, more a description of a community-based wise woman, who would prescribe remedies and simple charms for the benefit of her neighbours. She would have been well-versed in wort-lore and its various preparations; and although not to be recommended today without the proper training, she would have also been the local midwife. Much of what she needed could be found growing wild in the hedgerows, which also meant the parish-pump witch would have been familiar with the trees and plants that were to be found in her locality; and be aware of the changing of the seasons when different parts of the plant were best gathered. Like a well-washed rugby shirt, however, the demographics for describing the differences between parish-pump witchcraft, wise women and cunning ways blur into one another other with no clearly defined boundaries.

Part of the parish-pump witch's heritage would also have embraced the very real need for utilising wild food in order to supplement her meagre diet. It's easy to forget that every vegetable we use was once a wild plant and that many became a food source as a by-product of its medicinal use. The household hints are those that were in use for centuries in both grand country house and cottage alike, each having a reasonable plot of land on which to grow plants and vegetables for their needs. Although a wise woman wouldn't have differentiated between 'flowers' and 'herbs', *The Secret People* treats them as separate sections and defines herbs by their recognised culinary and healing properties. Where necessary the Latin names for plants have been included since many are known by other names in different parts of the country. For both healing and magical use it is essential that the correct plant be used, and therefore the Latin name ensures there is no confusion.

Hopefully *The Secret People* will prove useful to those pagans who repeatedly struggle to find an identity within contemporary paganism: to realise that it isn't necessary to adopt an inappropriate label in order to relate to the pagan lifestyle. Parish-pump witches and wise women were not witches in the traditional sense, but they *were* healers and charmers living semi-openly as useful members of the 'parish'. The cunning-folk often travelled about taking their healing around the countryside and using their skills to negate any malignant energies that might be afflicting their clients. Neither would necessarily have had any interest in the ritualised format and beliefs of traditional witchcraft.

Although *The Secret People* reflects traditions and customs that were usually thought of as a natural part of rural life, much of it can now be identified as integral elements of contemporary Wicca...but there is nothing in this book that cannot be transported into the towns and cities in order to make the urban witch's quest for his or her pagan identity a little easier and more enriching

Melusine Draco
Glen of Aherlow – 2016

Chapter One

The Gardener

Wort-lore or herbal healing was an area where *The Secret People* came into their own within the community, and it is also an area that doesn't require any particular magical skills. In other words, a considerable amount of wort-lore can be learned, rather than being seen as a natural ability. It has been said that domestic herbal medicine represents a 'home survival kit'; built up over the centuries through the daily life of ordinary people, it was preserved with remarkable accuracy from one generation to the next, well into the 20th century. Unfortunately, many of these simple, everyday natural remedies that were still in general use in our grandparents' time, are now in danger of disappearing altogether.

Perhaps it might be a good idea to begin by identifying what we mean by natural remedies and herbal medicine, because there is no standard definition of 'a herb'. Some will say that any useful plant is a herb; others only consider those used for culinary purposes deserve such recognition. Nevertheless, Nature has an impressive array of healing substances to be called upon, many of which have been scientifically acknowledged to be effective against many different ailments and bodily disorders.

It isn't enough, however, to *read* that rosemary can be used as a lotion applied to wounds, or that tea made with dried thyme cures a hangover. To get the most out of Nature's bounty, it is necessary to be familiar with the plants themselves; getting used to handling them and understanding how to make them thrive – sometimes in the most unlikely of places.

God of Small Spaces

Before getting down to the practical art of creating a witch's garden, however, it is important to define just how *small* the space available is for growing things. In today's social climate few are lucky enough to have large cottage gardens and most have to make do with an urban patch with neighbours in close proximity. Is the space as big as ten feet square, or not much wider than a side alley four feet deep? Is it a tiny yard, or a balcony area barely large enough for a plant pot? Even a paved patio can provide enough space to grow a number of different plants providing there is enough sun during the day.

In an urban environment light levels, climate, soil and boundaries are 'fixed', but even the darkest, tiniest of spaces can be turned into an attractive feature with a little bit of visualisation. No matter how small the area, think of it as an integral part of the home that can be enhanced to provide that oasis of calm in the middle of a town or city; in cases where privacy is threatened by being overlooked by neighbours the best plan may simply be to screen off as much as possible. Unsightly fences and walls can be covered with trellises to support scented climbers, but choose carefully to avoid problems of too much shade – unless the environment lends itself to a pergola to give screening from above.

By exploring the dozens of imaginative alternatives the urban wise woman can create her own outdoor environment in keeping with her lifestyle. Large mirrored sheets, for instance, are particularly effective when used to lengthen or widen a small area, while reflective materials such as polished or beaten metals produce a feeling of elemental fire. Brightly coloured plastic tubs can also transform a dull corner, especially if the area isn't suitable for flowers. No matter how gloomy the patch, ferns, hostas and ivy can still be used for maximum effect – as can wooden decking, pebbles and outside lighting.

Remember that any kind of window box, hanging basket, tub or container demands constant attention because the plants are entirely dependent on human care. Out in an open garden they can spread their roots in search of nourishment and moisture, but in the narrow confines of a small container they must be provided with everything they need. Very little rain falls straight down so even during wet weather window boxes and tubs may receive little or no moisture other than from a watering can. If ground space is limited, create a cascade of wall-mounted containers with trailing plants.

Just because the outside space is limited it doesn't mean a witch or wise woman can't create a small area of peace and calm with just a bit of careful planning. Before setting out the 'garden' area, mark the four cardinal points, or quarters. If it's big enough to stand in, it's big enough to use magically, so think about how a sacred area can be created that will mean nothing to any inquisitive neighbours. A simple method would be to use frost-resistant plaques, or small unobtrusive garden ornaments that symbolically represent the quarters.

Even a small space can provide space in which 'to be' and neighbours will think nothing if they see a person sitting on a step with a coffee, or relaxing in a garden chair in a special corner. Parish-pump witches, wise women and cunning ways do not require grand ritual gestures to follow their arte – a quiet corner prepared with loving care is the only space that is needed.

Flower Garden

At one time when *The Secret People* were the nearest any villager came to medical care, their gardens were always special places because they always needed ingredients for both spells and healing potions. Gardens, like homes, will take on an atmosphere or style of their owner, reflecting both the taste and personality of the one who cares for them. It is worth noting that many of the plants used in folk-medicine and magic are those that professional gardeners would class as weeds, as Rachel Patterson takes into account in *A Kitchen Witch's World of Magical Plants and Herbs.*

A contemporary witch's garden requires careful planning because it needs to contain plants to be used in personal magic, for healing purposes, and for sheer pleasure. The garden should be sensitive to the scale and mood of the surrounding landscape and buildings, so that the planting creates the privacy required, without overwhelming the space available for pleasure. It should also be borne in mind that a garden, however small, is a place to be used for magic, and this should be reflected in the layout.

Space permitting, a secluded corner should contain some sort of fire pit together with a moon-pool for scrying purposes. Depending on the size of the space available, the moon-pool in the form of a water feature can be placed in the centre of the garden; or a shallow bowl positioned at the western side, in its elemental quarter. Fire pits can be disguised as patio heaters or even the cut-off bottom of an LPG cylinder – both being ideal for a small garden. At night the fire is the gathering place where it can be used to brew potions, for scrying, to burn a magical Need Fire at the festivals – and a place to sit with friends, keep warm, eat, drink and gossip. Be aware, however, that in a built-up area, wind-chimes can constitute noise pollution if they annoy the neighbours!

Even the most modest of gardens can find room for fragrant bushes, plants and climbers. Large pots can be used to grow a rowan, or mountain ash – a small, decorative tree with white flowers in the spring and lovely red berries in the autumn. Place the pot at the boundary of the garden, or at one corner where it can watch over two boundaries and repel negative vibes. Rowan is extremely protective and its twigs are used to form crosses held together with red thread that will fend off any unwanted entities. This wood likes to be handled, so when pruning make the wood into a protective incense for burning on the open fire. It is said that to give your partner an object made of rowan wood is to ensure a happy and prosperous marriage...it can also be added to a binding if you are having problems with a straying spouse.

Miniature apple trees can be pot-grown on a patio, or trained as espaliers, a space-saving way of growing fruit on a south-facing wall or fence. They require little pruning once established, producing attractive blossom and fruit, and an architectural feature during winter. The fruit, blossom and wood can be used in many traditional spells – usually love charms, but also for protection and prosperity – and apple wood produces a wonderful perfume when burned on an open fire. An old super-stition says that it is lucky to leave an apple or two on the ground to keep any wandering Nature spirits happy. The old adage 'an apple a day keeps the doctor away' echoes the fruit's health-giving qualities for good skin, reducing cholesterol and combating allergies, asthma, gum disorders, heart disease and cancer. Dwarf holly trees can also be grown in small spaces since it is magically protective and sacred to the Horned God; if there is a rowan or apple (goddess) tree in the garden, it is a good idea to introduce a holly to keep the magical balance of energies.

Everyone has their favourite flowers and this should be a place of colour and fragrance – as well as for practical purposes. For fragrance, small bushes and shrubs such as honeysuckle, jasmine, lavender, mock orange and miniature lilac are best. Roses provide an ingredient in many love spells and are 'goddess flowers', as are all white lilies and sweet peas.

Rose Remedy

Rose honey is a traditional remedy for treating a sore throat.

Infuse two tablespoons of fresh rose petals in a cup of boiling water.

Cover and allow to cool. Strain the liquid and reheat with a spoonful of honey.

Allow to boil and pour into a heat-proof jar. Allow to cool before sealing.

Take a teaspoon and dilute in a little hot water.

Violet Remedy

For headaches, steep three teaspoons of fresh flowers and leaves (or one teaspoon of dried flowers) in a cup of boiling water.

Cover and allow to stand for fifteen minutes to infuse and cool.

Drink a cup daily or use as a cold compress.

When planning the garden, shrubs and plants should be chosen to provide colour and greenery all year round. As well as spring and summer colour, choose plants for autumn and winter interest since there is nothing more depressing than a large expanse of grass, bare borders or concrete. Hebes offer evergreen alternatives to conifers for small spaces, while the bark of dogwoods and cornelian cherry provide vibrant colour during the grey days of winter.

For purposes of tradition, this text confines itself to the plants, shrubs and foliage found in a typical cottage garden at the beginning of the 20th century. Although not a comprehensive list, these are some of the flowers our grandparents and great grandparents would have been familiar with throughout the seasons. Certain flowers were associated with birthdays, and became known as 'lucky flowers' – but these often vary from county to county. This list was taken from a 1930s edition of *The Woman's Treasury for Home and Garden*:

January (Snowdrops) and February (Primroses)

Since there is little available in the way of fresh flowers apart from red and yellow dogwood twigs, this is where stocks of dried flowers, seeds and grasses come into their own. Christmas roses are flowering in the garden, along with snowdrops which were believed to be harbingers of death [since they grew at Imbolc, the coldest time when stocks were running low and hunger took its toll]. Cornelian cherry, jasmine and viburnum are beginning to flower; while various forms of catkins can be brought into the house until their pollen begins to shed as this can mark furniture.

March (Daffodils)

Primroses and polyanthuses begin to bloom, together with crocuses and hellebores [avoid *heliborus foetidus* since its smell is singularly unpleasant in the confines of a room]. Ornamental almond, peach, plum, sloe and cherry trees flower early in the year to provide a splash of colour; as does the old favourite forsythia, which can be picked before the flowers bloom on the leafless stems. Anemones and celandines flower among the daffodils and narcissus in time for the Spring Equinox.

April (Daisies)

Forget-me-nots, primroses, polyanthus, violets and some early pansies add even more colour to the borders. Gardens with room for a variety of flowering shrubs will enjoy the beauty of japonica [also useful for its fruit], azaleas, rhododendrons, flowering currant and broom for Beltaine celebrations.

May (Lily-of-the-Valley)

This month sees the blaze of tulips mixed with late narcissus and lily-of-the-valley. With peonies and iris, aquilegia and poppies against a backdrop of trailing clematis Montana, spiraeas, mock orange and guelder rose.

June (Roses)

Roses take their place as 'queen of the garden' together with delphiniums, lupins, irises, marigolds, sweet peas and pinks – all ready in time for Summer Solstice.

July (Lilies)

Many of the flowers that started to bloom in June reach even more spectacular proportions this month, especially with roses, sweet pears, hollyhocks and stocks (*matthiola*). Marguerites and other daisy-shaped flowers are usually abundant for picking for indoor arrangements.

August (Gladioli)

Gladioli, montbretias, larkspur, asters and scabious, nasturtiums, dahlias, tamarisk and hydrangeas all add to the riot of colour in the garden at Lammastide before the evenings begin to cool.

September (Asters)

Sedum and dahlias come into their own, with chrysanthemums and asters gaining ground every day. Michaelmas daisies are a real sign that the Autumn Equinox is just around the corner.

October (Dahlias)

Snowberries and the cotoneasters produce a wild display of white and red berries, but from the gardener's point of view, summer is over as night mists, chilly winds and early frosts slow down production. A mix of autumn leaves with the last of the chrysanthemums provide a rich display for Samhain.

November (Chrysanthemums) and December (Holly)

Any indoor arrangements will now consist of bowls of variegated foliage, coloured twigs and browned beech leaves until the greenery is brought in for the Winter Solstice and Yule.

There are lots of superstitions attached to flowers, but most of them date from the Victorian era; although it is well to remember these when giving flowers to someone, especially if they are ill.

White flowers are taboo for a sick person, as are white and red mixes. Violet and blue flowers show goodwill and friendliness, while yellow and orange blooms represent warmth and the sun. It is unlucky for a sick person for flowers to be placed on the bed, and flowers should never be picked from a grave and then discarded, else the place where they fall will become haunted. Although flowers can brighten up a sick-room, heavy, cloying scents found in jasmine, hyacinths and lilies may be over-powering. There were even superstitions governing the placing of flowers on graves with sentimental meanings although the grave-tender's motto should be: 'A maximum quantity of evergreen to a minimum of coloured or pure white bloom.'

On a more up-beat note, flowers planted during the time of the new moon are said to bloom the best and sunflowers bring good luck to the whole garden. Lilac gets a mixed reception in different parts of the country. Some people claim it to be unlucky while others enjoy having large arrangements in the house. This superstition (according to family tradition) came into being during the English Civil War when lilac was the 'secret' symbol of the Royalists. Any Cavalier hiding from the Roundheads could safely claim sanctuary at a house displaying a bowl of lilac in the window; it would, however, have been unlucky for the family if the lilac was spotted by a passing troop of Parliamentarians who knew of its significance!

Pot marigolds are a good weather omen and if the flowers don't open before seven o'clock in the morning then a storm is in the offing. Marigolds were used in wedding garlands and love charms, and rubbing the juice from the head of the flower relieves the pain from a wasp or bee sting. Foxglove is a lovely flower that is still used medicinally as a heart tonic and is very poisonous – the extracted digitals being found in many commercial medicines. In the magic garden, however, it tells the Faere Folk and Nature spirits that they are welcome.

Lavender crops up all over the place and has so many uses it is difficult to know where to start. Not only does it provide a wonderful perfume and display of colour in the garden, it can also be put to good use within the home. Lavender is a most effective insect repellent and any sitting area should have a small hedge or tubs of the plant to keep summer flies and midges at bay. Bunches of lavender hanging indoors will also discourage insects from invading the house. For hundreds of years lavender has been used to perfume linen and laundry. Lavender pillows and cologne offer relief from tension, headaches and sleeplessness; lavender oil applied to small burns will relieve the pain and minimise scarring.

Flowers were also used in magical charms and the wise woman would have been well-versed in their use. For example:

Carnations (*dianthus cayophyllus*): If a girl-friend has been having a run of misfortune, give her a bunch of carnations, or Gilly-flowers, and this will turn her luck to good. Give a man a single flower to wear in his buttonhole for the same reason. Medicinally, they were used to alleviate malignant fevers, promote perspiration and quench raging thirsts.

Cornflowers (*cenaurea cyanus*): Dry some of the flowers and keep them in a bag by the hearth to bring harmony to your home. Medicinally, an infusion was used for digestive and gastric disorders. The petals were used to colour ink, cosmetics and medicines; it was also said to be a remedy against the poison of the scorpion, according to Culpeper!

Daisy (*bellis perennis*): The flowers themselves are believed to possess clairvoyant properties. Carry some in a pouch to increase your own psychic powers. Wear a daisy chain when you seek out the Faere Folk. Medicinally they were used in ointments to help heal wounds and bruises.

Foxglove (*digitals purpurea*): Make a tisane of the herb and add some to the water of other cut flowers to make them last longer, and bearing in mind the plant's poisonous nature, it was used medicinally in the treatment of heart disease and dropsy.

Heartsease (*viola tricolour*): Slip a few flowers in your lover's pocket to increase their desire for you and, ironically, it was used medicinally to treat venereal disease.

Marigolds (*calendula officinalis*): Make an infusion of marigold flowers and add this to the bath water. This will infuse your aura with golden light and increase your status in the eyes of the world. Do this whenever you need to enhance your charisma. To see your lover in a dream, stuff a walnut shell with marigold petals, seal the shell with red wax and wear it around your neck when you go to sleep. Medicinally, an infusion was used to soothe wasp and bee stings.

Plants and flowers are, in themselves, 'magical correspondences' and should be included in any magical operation, spell casting or charm – even if it's only a single blossom in a wine glass. The following are plants and flowers that correspond to the days of the week and their planetary associations:

Sunday/Sun: Ash, broom, acacia, bay vine – or any yellow flowers.

Monday/Moon: Jasmine, mandrake, orchid, eucalyptus, gardenia – or any white flowers.

Tuesday/Mars: Nettles, wormwood, red poppy – or any scarlet flowers.

Wednesday/Mercury: Mint, violet – or any flowers or leaves with a silvery effect.

Thursday/Jupiter: Opium poppy, lilac, clove, thistle – or any purple flowers.

Friday/Venus: Rose, foxglove, peach, rosemary – or any pink/pale mauve flowers.

Saturday/Saturn: Lotus, lily, belladonna, blackthorn – or any dark coloured flowers

To use flowers for a protective pouch, make a fresh one every year and burn the old one in the sacred fire. All the ingredients for the new one must be harvested and dried at the time of the full moon. Circle your cauldron chanting this traditional rhyme:

Round about the cauldron go
In! The herbs of magic throw,
Elfwort, trefoil, goat's leaf, bour,
In the cauldron the magic four.
Goatweed, basil, graveyard dust
Thrice about it go we must.
Elfleaf, dilly, Juno's tears,
Witchbane, bat's wings, dead men's bells
Together bind this magic spell.
Thrice about the cauldron run,
Charm the spell and it be done.

It isn't difficult to see how mysterious and exotic these ingredients would sound until it is revealed that they are the old names for plants used in spell-casting. For example, elfwort is elecampane, a member of the sunflower family and its use goes back to ancient Greece; goat's leaf is honeysuckle and bour is a 14th century name for elder flowers. Goatweed refers to St John's wort and 'graveyard dust' to valerian. Elfleaf refers to either rosemary or lavender and dilly is the herb dill; Juno's tears is vervain, witchbane is rowan, 'bat's wings' is holly and 'dead men's bells' is foxglove.

For all its magical properties, a flower garden *should* be an oasis of calm that reflects an individual style and feeling about the sensations that different colours and fragrances create. As well as taking the geographical factors into account, there is a need to arrange for the natural progression of colours and textures throughout the seasons because a garden can be a natural temple even against the backdrop of bricks and mortar in an urban winter landscape.

Herb Bed

As Robin Whiteman observed in *Brother Cadfael's Herb Garden*, the history of herbal medicine dates back to the dawn of time, when our ancestors realised that certain plants had a particular effect on their health and well-being. 'As magic and religion, biology and medicine, botany and philosophy all originally coexisted side by side (rather than being separate and distinct sciences), elaborate rituals grew up around the gathering and use of plants and herbs.'

The history of printed herbals stems largely from the manuscripts of Dioscorides (64AD), a Greek physician, and Pliny the Elder, a Roman naturalist, who died at Pompeii. In *De Materia Medica* (or the *Codex Vindobonensis*, dating from 512AD and the earliest surviving illustrated herbal in the western world) Dioscorides lists some 500 healing herbs, while the only work that remains of Pliny is his *Natural History* and the letters of his nephew, Pliny the Younger (62-111) who provides valuable information on plants and the layout of Roman gardens.

Galen (130-199) brought together the best knowledge of the Greek medical school (while striving to remove ritual and superstition), and classified herbs by their essential qualities of hot and cold, dry or moist, and strongly supported the theory of the four humours – blood, phlegm, black bile and yellow bile. The botanical works of Theophrastus (c372-287BC) were not translated into Latin until the 15th century, yet they became an important source of reference for many medieval herbalists and apothecaries.

In Britain, Benedictine monk Aelfric compiled his *Colloquy (Nominus Herbarum)* in 995AD that listed more than 200 herbs and trees. The Latin poem, *De virtutibus herbarum*, compiled in France in the first half of the 11th century was widely copied by hand throughout Europe; it was the first herbal to be printed in the western world in 1477. Although some of the secrets of the Physicians of Myddfai weren't written down until the 13th century, they provide a valuable source of information on Druidic herbal traditions – and reveal that the early Welsh physicians had a knowledge of Greek, Roman and Arabic plant and healing lore.

The earliest surviving Anglo-Saxon manuscript dealing with the virtues of herbs is the *Leech Book of Bald*, written by a Saxon doctor, or 'leech', in the early 10th century, embodying beliefs that dated back to primitive and mysterious times, long before the Romans and Christianity invaded the British Isles. The oldest illustrated herbal to have been preserved from Anglo-Saxon times is a translation of the Latin *Herbarum of Apuleius*, compiled in the 5th century. The *Lacnunga*, an Anglo-Saxon manuscript believed to date from the 10th century, contains a charm in praise of the nine sacred herbs of the Norse god Woden. These nine herbs that had powers over all manner of evils and poisons were mugwort, waybroad (plantain), stime (watercress), maythen (chamomile), wergulu (nettle), chervil, fennel, crab-apple and the unidentified 'atterlothe'.

The first printed English herbal, commonly known as *Bancke's Herbal*, was an anonymous compilation from various sources and was published in 1525 by Richard Bankes. William Turner's *A New Herbal*, which was published in three parts in 1551-68, marked the beginning of the science of botany in England; followed by *The Herbal, or Generall Historie of Plantes*, by John Gerard in 1597. Compiled by an apothecary, physician and astrologer, Nicholas Culpeper's *Complete Herbal and English Physician Enlarged* offered remedies for all ills known to the 17th century that had been used traditionally throughout Europe for 1,400 years. It also instructed the common people where to find the herbs and how to prepare the remedies for themselves.

Nowhere else in history, even to the present day, are *The Secret People* more at home than when working with herbs. There is no need, however, to have a grand herb garden such as the one the fictitious Brother Cadfael cultivated at Shrewsbury Abbey. Herbs can be grown in containers, a small patch of ground near the kitchen door, or be mixed with the flowers and vegetables in a border. Wort-lore was (and still is) the province of the true wise woman and none should be without a few essential herbs at her fingertips for both culinary and healing purposes, especially *'...parsley, sage, rosemary and thyme ...'* immortalised in the words of that classic English folk song, *Scarborough Fair*. And as Rachel Patterson comments in *A Kitchen Witch's World of Magical Plants and Herbs*: 'If you are able to grow herbs in your own garden, this is an excellent way of connecting with the magical energy as you follow the plant through its growth cycle.'

Parsley *(petroselinum crispum)*

In ancient times, both the Greeks and the Romans used parsley in their funerary rites. Thus connection with death may account for the old British superstition that the herb should always be home-grown and never given or received as a gift since the recipient would inherit all the domestic problems and ill-luck of the giver. In some rural communities it is also considered back luck or dangerous to transplant or even move a parsley bed. Turner's *New Herbal* (1904 reprint) claimed that: *'The sede taken beforehand helpeth men that have weyke braynes to beare drinke better.'* Culpeper

(1653) wrote that the distilled water was given to both adults and children troubled by wind in the belly. The herb was also listed by Aelfric (995) in his *Colloquy* (*Nominum Herbarum*). Apart from its culinary uses, raw parsley is still an efficient breath-freshener, particularly after eating garlic. In the past it was prescribed for menstrual problems, urinary infections, coughs and eye complaints – and even as a poultice for treating cuts, sprains and insect bites. Parsley was thought to be an antidote to poison and that to sprinkle the herb on a dish as a garnish was seen as a sign of good faith.

Magical use: Carried for personal protection in both this and Otherworld; also used in rites of purification.

Sage (*salvia offininalis*)

Sage is another herb considered sacred by the Greeks, and according to the Romans, the herb should not be cut with an iron knife as sage reacts to iron salts. In English superstition it is believed to be a lucky plant, able to impart wisdom and to strengthen the memory. It was also said that if sage grew in profusion in any garden then a woman of strong will lived there.

Sage was viewed as a 'cure all' and is wonderfully antiseptic if used to make gargles for sore throats and to freshen the breath. It is also widely used in cookery, and goes well with pork. Try it as a hors d'oeuvre simply dipped in batter and deep fried – it is deliciously different and inexpensive to prepare.

Magical use: It is used to evoke wisdom, to reveal secrets, and to help a witch keep her wits about her. It is also reputed to possess the power of longevity and to strengthen mental powers.

Rosemary (*rosemarinus officinalis*)

Worn by the Greeks to aid memory, rosemary was introduced into Britain by the Romans. Among the many curious superstitions is that it will only grow where a woman is head of the household (either literally or figuratively). A symbol of friendship, loyalty and remembrance, rosemary is traditionally carried by mourners at a funeral, and a bride at her wedding. It was also believed that spoons made of the wood cause even the blandest food to taste good – just as combs made of it will make hair grow according to French custom. *Banckes's Herbal* (1525) advised that smelling a box of rosemary wood *'shall preserve thy youth'*. Small amounts of crushed rosemary dropped into a barrel of beer will prevent all who drink from it from getting drunk – but extremely large doses can be poisonous.

A 17th century tea

1 teaspoon of rosemary leaves
2 teaspoons of lemon balm leaves
6 teaspoons of rose leaves
A handful of rose petals

Chop finely once dried and brew as usual.

A pillow of rosemary and lavender will soothe headaches, relieve stress and bring restful sleep: *'Add some thyme and your dreams will be magical.'* (*A Witch's Treasury for Hearth & Garden*).

Magical use: To banish illness from a house, and carried for purification and protection; also used in rites of exorcism and banishment, and to strengthen mental powers.

Thyme (*thymus vulgaris*)

Thyme was used by both the Egyptians and the Etruscans for embalming their dead. The herb has retained its associations with death and Otherworld; the flowers provided a resting place for the spirits of the departed and the smell of thyme has apparently been detected at several haunted sites. The Faere Folk are said to love thyme and are believed to dance upon it to release the fragrance. Used as an antiseptic and a disinfectant, thyme was also used in soaps, cosmetics, perfumes and potpourri. Its culinary use helped the digestion of fatty meats such as mutton and pork, as well as adding flavour to soups, stews, stuffings and other dishes.

Magical use: Use for healing workings, purification and cleansing. A prepared pouch of thyme gives courage to the bearer and is used in rites of purification.

Start with one natural remedy or multi-purpose herb at a time. Experiment and get a *feel* for each individual plant and all its uses, so that preparation comes automatically. Begin with the four listed above since all can be obtained ready-grown in pots from a supermarket or garden centre until your own home-grown plants mature. Needless to say, these particular herbs have been around for a very long time. Parsley is still used as a digestive aid and was said to 'take away bitterness'; medieval doctors prescribed it for spiritual maladies as well. Sage has been a symbol of strength for thousands of years; while rosemary represents faithfulness, love and remembrance. Thyme symbolises courage, and during the Middle Ages ladies presented their 'favours' embroidered with a sprig of thyme to their chosen knight.

A gift of 'parsley, sage, rosemary and thyme' is also ideal for a simple and inexpensive wedding, birthday or house-warming present. Depending on the season, replant commercially bought herbs in gaily coloured individual containers with a matching water tray for the kitchen window sill. Or plant up a window box, keeping the herbs in their pots (as this will prevent the roots from taking over the container) and add a few nasturtium seeds in the compost between the pots for colour. The addition of a suitable book such as the *RHS Encyclopaedia of Herbs and Their Uses* makes this a highly personal gift for a close friend or relative.

Even with the minimal amount of space, these 'famous four' can also be grown quite successfully in outdoor pots and containers. Space permitting, however, a wise woman's garden can also include the following for planting in the flower beds and borders. The Latin names listed in this section are those of the medieval varieties given in *Brother Cadfael's Herb Garden*:

Bay (*laurus nobilis*)

The bay (or sweet laurel) was dedicated to Apollo and his son, Aesculapius, the god of medicine. During the Middle Ages it was predominantly used as a 'strewing' herb because of its fragrance and also its insect-repelling properties. Because it is an evergreen, bay can be used to flavour soups and stews all the year round. Bay trees can be as large or small as you choose, with tiny 'kitchen' bays for windows sills available from garden centres and supermarkets.

Magical use: A bay, no matter how small, should be part of every witch's defence system as a vital ingredient against malignant forces and psychic attack; also an important ingredient in purification rites.

Chives (*allium schoenoprasum*)

Chives are used for flavouring, to soothe inflammation and insect bites, although they are rarely used medicinally. They add bite to potato, cheese, egg and salad dishes where the use of onions or shallots would be too overpowering. The pretty mauve flowers make them ideal for a border plant. Although this herb was found in a medieval garden there is little recorded about it except that it was for flavouring and to treat insect bites and inflammation. The herb was known in medieval times, but only briefly mentioned by Culpeper.

Magical use: None found.

Comfrey (*miniature symphytum officinale*)

This plant should be kept in every garden (in dwarf variety), the original being brought to England by the Crusaders from the

Holy Land. Bearing in mind its very intrusive nature, plant it in a container or to the back of the border in a moist place as it likes to grow in dykes and ditches. Cut it often for 'instant' compost, or let it flower for the bees and cut it back in the autumn. It produces nitrogen, so even if there isn't a compost heap, use it to mulch around plants that need feeding. Use the sap neat on wounds (the herb is also known as knitbone) and a poultice of the herb will dry out to form a version of a vegetable plaster. Culpeper also recommended the plant for sore breasts and haemorrhoids (*The English Physician Enlarged*, 1653), for which purpose it is still used by the pharmaceutical industry today. The roots and leaves of comfrey were used in numerous herbal preparations, but the most common use is in its healing properties for bruises, wounds and strains. **Not to be taken internally**.

Hair restorer recipe

Chop up some comfrey leaves and seal them in a jar. Leave this for 1-2 years and at the end of this time all that remains is an oily viscous liquid. This can be used on the head daily as a hair restorer and as a very potent wound healer, but if the idea doesn't appeal it can be used on indoor plants as a fertiliser!

Magical use: To gain riches or wealth, and to use as protection while travelling.

Feverfew (*chrysanthemum parthenium* or *tanacetum parthenium*)
Mainly used to reduce fevers and cure migraines, feverfew is said to relieve arthritic pains if a fresh leaf is eaten every day, although over-use can cause dermatitis and mouth ulcers. One of the new varieties with golden leaves and small daisy-like flowers makes an ideal plant for the flower border. It was an important 16th century 'strewing' herb, the dried flowers retaining their insecticidal properties almost indefinitely.

Magical use: For use as a protective herb during pregnancy and childbirth; and to maintain general health and longevity.

Garlic (*allium sativum*)

The use of garlic to ward off evil spirits can be traced back to Egypt and Babylon, although it has always been recognised for both its culinary and medicinal qualities. It would probably be easier to list what garlic *isn't* good for since it has the highest therapeutic value of all the onion family, including being considered a rejuvenative, detoxicant and aphrodisiac in Ayurvedic medicine.

Magical use: The leaves, flowers and cloves are used in exorcisms and banishment.

Houseleek (*sempervivum tectorum*)

This plant was used 2,000 year ago for treating ulcers, burns, scalds and inflammations. It was also used for soothing skin rashes, stings, insect bites, and to remove warts and corns. Believed by the Greeks and Romans to prevent lightning strikes if grown on the roof of a house; the plant was introduced into Britain by the Romans and its young, evergreen leaves were added to salads or eaten as a vegetable. The Anglo-Saxons knew it as *leac*.

Magical use: Charlemagne ordered that it be grown throughout his empire for its magical properties, which included keeping 'witches and evil spirits' away, i.e. negative energies.

Mint (*menthe spicata*)

Mint is a very versatile herb and a herb garden should contain several different varieties. Spearmint is the ordinary garden mint (commonly used for mint sauce to serve with lamb); **peppermint** (*menthe piperita*) makes cooling tisanes and helps breathing for colds and flu. One of the most powerful of the mint family is **pennyroyal** (*menthe pulegium*), but care should be taken when using it since it can bring on menstruation and was used by 'incautious young women' to encourage abortion. Traditionally it was used to repel mice and insects, but bees love pennyroyal and if it is grown near a hive, bees will not desert the colony. Bees also like **lemon balm** (*melissa officinalis*), which is also known as 'bee balm' and even its Latin name *melissa* means bee. Grow it for its delicious smell and flavour: put fresh leaves under the skin of a chicken and when it is cooked the meat will have a lovely lemony flavour. Mint, with its antiseptic, anti-bacterial, anti-spasmodic and anti-inflammatory properties, has dozens of uses, not to mention its value in the kitchen. It should be grown in tubs or containers as it is extremely invasive and will quickly overcrowd other plants.

Magical use: Watermint (*menthe aquatica*) was one of the three most sacred herbs of the Druids (the other two being meadowsweet and vervain). Both peppermint and lemon balm were used for their ability to defuse anger and spearmint (*menthe spicata*) strengthens mental powers and offers protection. Peppermint (*menthe piperita)* strengthens psychic powers and is used in rites of purification.

Periwinkle or **Sorcerer's Violet** (*vinca major*)
This is a pretty ground-cover plant, and also known as *priapiscus*, sacred to the god Priapus because of the phallic shaped buds. Although it has many medicinal uses, the plant can be poisonous.

Magical use: The old grimoires say it should be plucked when the moon is new, or when it is nine or thirteen nights old, to the chant of:

> *I pray thee, Vinca Pervinca, thee that art to be*
> *Had for thy many useful qualities, that thou*
> *Come to me glad, blossoming with all thy manfulness;*
> *That thou outfit me so that I be shielded and*
> *Prosperous, and undamaged by poisons and wrath.*

Dry the herb and use it for protection in rites of conjuration –

grow it in the garden to protect borders, repel demons and dispel the envy of others. As a symbol of immortality, it was linked with death and often worn by those about to be executed.

Rue (*ruta graveolens*)

Rue is said to possess curative properties, particularly for the eyes and in superstition the rue plant symbolises regret and repentance. For culinary usage, rue has a strong aromatic flavour but it is an 'acquired' taste.

Magical use: In Britain people would throw a handful of the herb at someone who had wronged them with the curse: *'May you rue the day as long as you live!'* Together with a sprig of rosemary, it will ensure that the guilty party never forgets their ill-deed. In Italy, witches wear a special amulet called a *cimaruta*, which means 'sprig of rue', fastened with little charms. Rue is also used in rites of banishing and exorcism, to get rid of negative entities, to break bewitchments (it was said to be the plant Odysseus used to counter the charms of Circe). The Romans believed its regular consumption could give second sight and both Leonardo de Vinci and Michelangelo are said to have taken it for its vision-enhancing powers. It was also associated with the god Pan, and a sprig worn in the button hole is believed in many places to keep off evil spells; it is also used in spells of exorcism and banishment, to stop gossip and strengthen mental powers.

St John's Wort (*hypericum pergoratum*)

One of the few indigenous herbs, St John's wort, or *hypericum*, is another protective herb, and there are many varieties to choose from, including the large and blowsy rose of Sharon. It was widely used for external treatment of wounds – particularly deep sword cuts. Despite its ancient use in medicine, the plant has gained quite a modern reputation as a treatment against depression, stress and even unhappiness – being described as Nature's Prozac!

Magical use: The yellow flowers should be picked around the Summer Solstice although superstition says that those treading on the plant after sunset would be carried away by a fairy-horse for a wild journey lasting the entire night. It is said to protect against melancholy and madness, and to aid in divination and love spells.

Any healer will constantly add to their collection of herbs as they find unusual varieties that appeal to them, such as Grim the Collier with its bright orange flowers. Or Good King Henry, also known as Lincolnshire spinach and grown as a pot-herb in that county as a wonderful antibiotic to use as a poultice on wounds, sores and ulcers. Lady's mantle, traditionally known as 'woman's best friend' was used for treating female complaints. It was said to possess magical powers on account of the way water settles on the leaves and this dew-fall or 'celestial water' was used by medieval alchemists.

Mugwort and wormwood are both known as 'bitter herbs' because of their strong flavour, but both have been added to alcoholic drinks: mugwort to beer (hence its name) and wormwood to the infamous absinthe (which is both its French and Latin name). Mugwort, one of the nine sacred herbs of the Anglo Saxons, was also used to strengthen clairvoyant powers, so a little should be carried in a pouch around the neck. A sprinkling of mugwort on tarot cards or a crystal ball is said to increase the accuracy of the reading.

Wormwood incense is used to raise the spirits of the dead, and should be an ingredient of Samhain incense to ensure the attendance of the denizens from beyond the veil. A native plant of Europe and Asia, wormwood was highly prized by many ancient civilisations, including the Egyptians, Greeks and Romans. Wormwood was also used as an aromatic ingredient in perfumed oils for the lamps, and although pillows stuffed with wormwood were recommended for insomnia, over-use of the herb can be extremely dangerous.

According to Paul Huson in *Mastering Herbalism*, the nine sacred herds, recorded since Anglos-Saxon times, are plantain, nettle, mugwort, coxspur grass, chamomile, apple, watercress, thyme and fennel. Plantain, nettle and couch (or coxspur) grass are today considered to be weeds. Plantain (fleawort) was used medicinally, some plants were used for their leaves and others for their seeds, while couch grass was included in many preparations for the treatment of bowel and kidney infections. In medieval times, fennel seeds were used as flavouring and eaten during Lent to allay hunger; watercress is rich in vitamins and minerals including iron, iodine, and calcium; chamomile tea remains a popular tisane for sleeplessness.

Two very poisonous plants are belladonna (aka *dwale* and deadly nightshade), and aconite (aka monkshood and wolfsbane). Both these plants have been given as ingredients of witches' flying ointment, the salve that was rubbed all over the body to make the user think they were flying to a Sabbat. It is interesting that each is said to be the antidote for the other; if anyone was foolish enough to eat belladonna, the antidote to the poison would be aconite, and vice versa. Used together in flying ointment it is speculated that the combination would give the hallucinogenic effect of flight, combined with the paralysis of the body that would prevent 'sleep walking'. Providing they are kept well away from children and animals, grow them for their curiosity value and because they are unusual and beautiful plants.

The best herbs for drying and storing for use during the winter months are basil, marjoram, rue, mint, sage, summer savoury, tarragon and thyme. It is important that herbs to be used for this purpose should be gathered at just the right time or they will certainly lose much of their aromatic properties. *The Secret People* know that leaves should be harvested before any seeds appear since the fading of the flowers synchronises with the waning of the potency in the leaves. The flavouring and magical properties are at their highest when the blossoms are just approaching their full display.

The actual task of harvesting consists of merely cutting the stems with a sufficient length of stalk for ease of handling. It is a common mistake to make a big bundle and tie them so tight that the centre generates a certain amount of heat so that discolouration or even mould spoils the leaves. Small open bunches enables the leaves to dry without loss of flavour or aroma. The greatest mistake of all is to dry the leaves in scorching sunlight or in an oven as this is sufficient to ruin them completely.

The best method is to hang them up in a dry place where there is a constant current of air. After a week or ten days examine them for any signs of decay or fungus; when they are sufficiently dry and crisp, the leaves will separate from the stalks under the slightest pressure. Leave them for a couple of days in a dry atmosphere and then bottle. As long as air is excluded, the herbs will be in a fit condition to use for a number of years, providing jars or bottles are tightly closed down after each opening.

For magical purposes, herbs should be gathered in order to preserve the highest concentration of the plant's qualities. There are traditional rules for gathering, although certain plants have their own specific ritual instructions. In some cases, these rules apply only to herbs gathered for a specific purpose (or spell); in others they refer to the way in which a certain herbs should be handled to maintain its maximum magical 'charge'. One frequent instruction, for example, is that the plant should be gathered without the touch of iron – and it has been confirmed by scientific experiment that certain trace elements and minerals found in some plants can be distorted, or even destroyed, by iron.

Even the most elementary study of plants and folklore reveals that there are a large number of plants that are traditionally associated with 'the Devil' for one reason or another. With some, all that remains of the Devil is part of the plant's name, but with others there are specific legends to explain these associations. This was an obvious attempt to 'demonise' certain plants that were important to the wise woman's trade, and no doubt has something relating to the plant's significance in pre-Christian beliefs or practices.

Many are often related to parts of the Devil's anatomy. For example: Devil's beard is another name for the antirrhinum (or snapdragon); American wake robin is known as Devil's ears; Devil's eye is an alternate name for henbane – another highly poisonous plant that crops up as an ingredient of witches' flying ointment, possibly for its hallucinogenic properties. Another poisonous, hallucinogenic plant (*datura stramonium*) is known as Devil's apples while belladonna (*atropa belladonna*) has two names – Devil's herb and Devil's cherries, due to its tempting fruit that has often killed children in the past.

Bindweed (*convolvulus*) is also known as Devil's intestines and an orchid (*dactylorhiza incarnate*) is called Devil's hoof. The fruit of the true mandrake (*mandragora officinarum*) is the Devil's testicles, and the stinkhorn fungus (*phallus iinpudicus*) is affectionately known as Devil's dick. There is also Devil's dung (*asafoetida ferrula*), probably because of its appalling and highly penetrating stench; a substance some herbalists refuse to stock because its invasive smell pervades everything around it. By contrast, asafoetida is a well-known ingredient in Indian cookery, and also known as 'the food of the gods'.

One of the best known of the Devil's plants is Devil's bit scabious. The root of this plant terminates abruptly, giving the impression that it has been bitten off, and according to legend the Devil was so annoyed with the plant because of its healing properties, that he tried to kill it by biting off the root. The seed cases of the honesty flower are known as Devil's ha'penny – when they still have their dried, protective covers; when the seeds are shed and the delicate satin-white inner casing is revealed, they are known as fairy silver.

Yarrow is another plant associated with the Devil due to its many magical properties, or because of its importance to our pagan ancestors. It is known both as Devil's nettle and Devil's plaything, probably because of its wide usage in spells and divination. Reference is found to this usage in both Celtic and Anglo-Saxon writings and the following charm should be recited as the yarrow stalk is picked in order to make the practitioner more sexually attractive:

I will pick the smooth yarrow
that my figure may be more elegant,
that my voice may be more cheerful;
may my voice be like a sunbeam,
may my lips be like the juice of strawberries.
May I be an island in the sea,
may I be a hill on the land,
may I be a star when the moon wanes,
may I be a staff to the weak one:
I shall wound every man,
No man shall wound me!

Other plants that are associated with the Devil, if not named after him, include wormwood that is said to have sprung up along the track made by the Devil as he slithered out of Eden in the form of a serpent. Wormwood was believed to be so potent that it could counteract the poison of hemlock, the bite of a shrew-mouse, or a sea-dragon!

An entire herb collection can consist of pots and containers on walls, steps and window sills, and almost any type of container is suitable, proving it will allow for drainage. Small herb collections can be assembled in the spring and planted in a variety of containers since most herbs will rub along quite nicely together. Although terracotta pots are everyone's first choice, they dry out too quickly in warm weather and are liable to crack if left out over winter. Strawberry pots of all sizes can achieve a remarkable effect once the herbs begin to grow; nasturtiums also look good in these containers and the leaves will provide a peppery flavour for salads. Suggested herbs and plants for containers are:

Trailing Herbs
Basil thyme (*acinos arvensis*)
Scotch broom (*cytisus*)
Wild strawberry (*fragaria vesca*)
Ivy (*hedera helix*)
Rosemary (*rosmarinus officinalis* 'Prostratus')
Thyme (*thymus serpyllum*)
Nasturtium (*tropaeolum*)
Periwinkle (*vinca minor*)

Compact Herbs
Mountain box (*hebe buxifolia*)
Common box or Kingsville dwarf (*buxus microphylla*)
Chinese pinks (*dianthus chinensis*)
Ivy (*hedera helix erecta*)
Hyssop (*hyssopus officinalis*)
Lavender (*lavandula officinalis*)
Dwarf myrtle (*myrtus communis compacta*)
Basil (*mini purpurascens* or 'Wellsweep' and 'minimum')
Marjoram (*compactum*)
Tricolour sage (*salvia officinalis* 'Tricolour')
Dwarf mountain pine (*pinus mugo*)
Cotton lavender (*santolina chamaecyparissus*)
Houseleek (*sempervivum*)
French marigolds (*tagetes patula*)
Thyme (*thymallus* various)

Wort-lore isn't just about knowing which herbs are suitable for

use in treating medical conditions, it is also about their history, superstitions, magical use and correspondences.

Vegetable Plot

Nowadays, few people have gardens big enough to grow large crops of vegetables, but few will also deny the sheer luxury of eating those first new potatoes, radishes, tomatoes and lettuces. Today it is seen as fashionable to grow salad vegetables in flower borders; potatoes can be cultivated in tubs; runner beans with their beautiful scarlet blossoms can be trained along a trellis, while small tomatoes are grown in hanging baskets. This modest vegetable plot won't reduce house-keeping bills, but it will provide a sense of achievement in growing some of the family's food. In addition, freshly picked produce has more flavour, a better texture and is richer in vitamin C – and therefore much healthier. *The Secret People* have always known that freshly picked vegetables in the diet can make an enormous difference to an individual's health.

If 'growing your own' is not realistic, the increasing popularity of farmers' markets springing up around the country now makes it possible to enjoy fresh vegetables straight from the land rather than the sterile, pre-packed, chill-stored produce from supermarkets. Fresh vegetables provide a healthy diet and supply the essential vitamins and minerals to help combat an increasing number of illnesses and diseases such as cancer and coronary complaints.

Using fresh vegetables does, of course, mean that they must be prepared in time-honoured fashion and acceptance of the fact that they come with the 'livestock' normally associated with garden-fresh produce.

Preparation and Cooking

All green vegetables should be washed well in salted water, as salt brings out the aphids, slugs and caterpillars that maintain a tenacious hold if only fresh water is used. A wise woman knows that if vegetables are cut early in the morning with the dew still on them and kept in a cold place until required, they will retain their original freshness. Cut in the heat of the day and having spent hours in a warm place, they can be revived by being put to soak in a bowl of cold water after washing and before cooking.

Peeled, sliced and chopped potatoes should be placed in cold water for five minutes to remove the starch from the cut surfaces. If this is not done, the starch grains will cloud the water used for cooking and often cause burning. Potatoes should not be peeled long in advance of cooking; if left covered with water some types of potato will taste watery when cooked.

The water in which vegetables are cooked should almost always be boiling before they are put in, but there are a few exceptions to this rule. Potatoes are traditionally put into cold water; beetroot can be placed in either cold or warm water. All green vegetables, including peas, beans, asparagus, leeks, cauliflower and broccoli, should be boiled with the saucepan lid *off* in order to keep the colour. If they are steamed, overcooked, or boiled with the lid on the saucepan, the steam is trapped and the vegetables turned a yellowish colour.

A small amount of salt can be added to the water used for boiling vegetables, as it improves the flavour and, in the case of green vegetables, prevents loss of colour to a certain extent by raising the boiling point of the water before they are added. In the 'good old days' bicarbonate of soda was used, but it was discovered that it destroys vitamin C and even ruins saucepans! Sweet vegetables, such as peas, asparagus, carrots and turnips, are improved by the addition of a teaspoon of sugar to the water. Root vegetables should be cooked with the lid *on* the saucepan.

All green vegetables of the cabbage family should be boiled rapidly and not allowed to come off the boil. Country-lore says that a crust of bread or a piece of toast placed in the water will absorb some of the smell associated with boiled cabbage. All vegetables, other than green ones, can be steamed and all vegetables should be drained immediately they are cooked. The valuable salts in the water can be utilised by saving the liquid to make into gravy, or added to soup stock. This water should not be mixed with meat stock until the soup is being made, or the meat stock will turn sour.

For many years it was believed that boiling destroyed vitamins in vegetables, but the pendulum has swung back again since it has been discovered that boiling *releases* the goodness. Yesterday's magic has always been looked upon as today's science, and scientific analysis shows increasingly more and more what parents and grandparents having been saying for years – that eating vegetables *is* good for you.

For example: carrots may not enable us to see in the dark, but they can help combat cancer, while a regular diet of cabbage and cauliflower slows down memory loss as we grow older. Even Brussels sprouts, kale and broccoli can help lower the risk of cancer; as do celery, spinach, peas and turnips. Onions (including garlic and chives) are thought to have an effect on Alzheimer's, cancer and heart disease. Sweet peppers and tomatoes may aggravate an arthritic condition, but both lessen the risk of cancer.

A well-balanced diet of correctly prepared and cooked vegetables can add to the quality of life now and in the future. It might even encourage veggi-phobes in children to enjoy fresh vegetables compared to the water-laden products often found in supermarkets under the heading of 'fresh vegetables'.

Growing Your Own
Anyone can grow vegetables if they follow the instructions and apply common sense. After all, as *The Secret People* are aware, it is in the natural order of things for seeds to germinate and develop into fully-grown plants. Even if there has been trial and error in the past, there could be several reasons for the failure and

obviously vegetables cannot grow in water-logged soil or excessive shade. Perhaps the plot wasn't provided with sufficient fertiliser, or maybe the seeds were sown at the wrong time, sown too close together, or seedlings weren't thinned out enough.

Autumn and winter are the best times to make a start and in a small garden every bit of space counts. Limited space dictates that vegetables also be integrated into the flower border, or grown in various sized tubs and containers. If there is space, raised beds can be installed to provide the depth required for growing 'green' or root vegetables. There is now a variety of miniature and dwarf vegetables that are good for container growing and apart from spacing and often early harvesting, normal growing practices apply. Miniature vegetables, such as beans, beetroot, cabbage, carrots, melons, corn, cucumbers, aubergines, lettuces, onions, peas, potatoes and tomatoes have the same soil, water, nutrient, and light requirements as ordinary varieties.

Most country people believe plants and seeds are best sown when the moon is waxing – except for plants like runner beans and peas that twine themselves around poles in an anti-clockwise (deosil) direction, and should be sown when the moon is waning. For magical and medicinal use of vegetables consult *Herbs: Medicinal, Magical, Marvellous!* by Deborah J Martin for help in identifying those Latin names for the correct plant and its magical attributes.

Space-Saving Vegetables

Lettuce
For the small garden, dwarf cos lettuce is easy to grow in almost any soil, providing it is enriched with compost and plenty of water. Try it served with a sour cream dressing as a light lunch with crusty bread.

Lettuce with Soured Cream Dressing
2 lettuces
1 each red and green pepper
2 hard boiled eggs
1 clove garlic
4 tablespoons olive oil
1 tablespoon white wine vinegar
2 tablespoons soured cream
Salt and pepper to taste

Use whole lettuce leaves to line a bowl and shred the rest. Mix shredded lettuce with the peppers and place in the bowl.
Remove the yolks from the hard boiled eggs and mash with a fork. Blend in the crushed garlic and stir in the other ingredients until smooth. Season to taste. Pour soured cream dressing over the salad and garnish with the chopped egg whites.

History: The Egyptians, Greeks and Romans all credited lettuce with magical properties, believing it to be a protection against drunkenness as well as an aphrodisiac. The wild lettuce was different to those known today; due to its narcotic effect it was known as the 'poor man's opium'. The medieval lettuce was bitter in taste and either cooked as a vegetable, or added to pottage and soups. As a salad vegetable it came into its own at the court of Louis XIV during the 16th century.

Magical use: Wild lettuce (*lactuca virosa*) was used in spells to preserve chastity; for rites of protection and to aid divination, particularly in matters of romance.

Onions

In a restricted space the only onions suitable for growing are spring onions and chives. Chives need little attention and are certainly among the easiest of garden plants to grow. Fresh clumps can be created every few years by lifting and dividing the existing ones. Spring onions and chives add bite to salads, omelettes and stir fry dishes.

History: The onion was one of the first plants to be cultivated across the ancient world, and valued for both its culinary and medicinal use by the Egyptians, Sumerians, Greeks and Romans. Possibly brought to Britain by the Crusaders, in medieval times onions were either dried or pickled for winter use; chives were mentioned by Culpeper in *The Complete Herbal* in 1649.

Magical use: Onions (*allium cepa*) were used in rites of protection, exorcism or banishment; to promote healing and encourage lust; attract wealth and riches and to cause prophetic dreams.

Potatoes

Not generally suitable for small gardens, it is possible to produce a small amount for special occasions using a barrel. This means a modest crop can be grown for the first taste of new potatoes, or for a family treat at Yule, since home-grown new potatoes have an unequalled flavour all of their own. New potatoes should be scrubbed or scraped – never peeled – or boiled in their skins.

New Potatoes to Cook

The vegetables should be freshly dug as they lose flavour once they are out of the ground. Put into boiling water with a couple of sprigs of fresh mint. Boil until tender when pierced with a fork; drain and leave to dry before adding butter mixed with fresh parsley.

History: Originally brought over from the New World in 1536 after the Spanish conquered Peru and carried them to Europe; by 1600 use of the vegetable had spread across Europe.

Magical use: Potatoes (*solanum tuberosum*) were used in later spells to promote healing.

Radish

In Shakespeare's day they were a favourite dish to stimulate the appetite; from a medicinal viewpoint they were used to treat respiratory and bronchial complaints, while in the kitchen they were eaten raw, or put in sauces and stews. For a continuous supply of summer radishes sow a row every three weeks; serve with crusty bread and salt as an appetiser. The large-rooted winter variety can be cooked like turnips and served with parsley sauce.

History: Several different varieties of radish were known to the ancient Egyptians, Greeks and Romans, although by Anglo-Saxon times the radish was so plentiful in the wild that they were seldom cultivated in England.

Magical use: Radishes (*raphanus sativus*) were used in spells to increase lust and in rites of protection.

Tomato

Tomatoes are a relative newcomer to the cottage garden, but new varieties make it possible to cultivate an ongoing crop throughout the summer without the use of a greenhouse. Tomatoes need the maximum amount of sun and water – and a regular feeding if they are to provide a continuous summertime crop. There are now several varieties that can be grown in containers, hanging baskets and window boxes, and still provide a large amount of small, tasty fruit.

Tomato Salad

Slice the tomatoes and add a tablespoon of spring onions or chives to each serving, and a teaspoon of chopped basil. Sprinkle with black pepper and balsamic vinegar. Serve with crusty bread for a light summer lunch.

History: Tomatoes originated from South America and were first cultivated by the Aztecs and Incas as early as 700AD. Tomatoes didn't arrive in Europe until the 16th century. Until the end of the 19th century most Europeans avoided eating them because of the belief that they caused sickness and death. The reason was that wealthy Europeans used pewter plates to serve food, which contained high lead content and because tomatoes are naturally very acidic, when placed on pewter platters the fruit would leach lead, which often resulted in terminal lead poisoning!

Magical use: Tomatoes (*solanum lycopersicum*) were used in later spells to attract love and obtain prosperity.

Decorative Vegetables

Beans

Beans or 'pulses' comprised the staple diet in medieval England and were dried to make a thick, starchy soup known as pottage; in the Middle Ages they were used in the form of a poultice to reduce inflammations and swellings. Broad beans can be grown at the back of the border in November for an early crop, or in March/April for the main crop. A double bonus means that the tops can be picked and cooked like spinach. Young broad beans are best served with butter and black pepper, while an older crop is delicious with fresh parsley sauce.

Broad Beans with Parsley Sauce
2 pints young broad beans
2 tablespoons fresh parsley
Half pint of parsley sauce

Once the beans are cooked, drain and pour over the sauce, adding the fresh parsley before serving. Perfect for an accompanying vegetable or as a light lunch eaten with crusty bread.

Originally from South America, runner beans with their glorious display of scarlet flowers can be used to create a variety of screening and other ornamental effects, as well as providing a delicious vegetable. Growing to over six feet high, they can be grown on wigwams, on tripods, netting, or twined around individual or sloping poles. They prefer rich, well-prepared soil, plenty of water and a site well out of the wind. Plants can be grown from seed or purchased from a garden centre. A dwarf variety of French bean is low-growing and only needs the support of twiggy sticks. The leaves are small and the sweet pea-like flowers come in a range of colours, depending upon the variety. French beans grow best in well-drained, light, but rich soil in a sunny position.

History: Evidence of broad beans in Britain has been found dating back to the Iron Age and possibly earlier and they were an important source of protein throughout Old and New World history.

Magical use: None found.

Beetroot

Humans originally ate beet greens, but not the thin and fibrous roots, which were occasionally used in medicine. The colourful, sweet root vegetable known as the beet tends to spark an impassioned response from folks who either love it or loathe it. The white beetroot was used medicinally for headaches and giddiness; the red was said to 'stay the bloody flux, women's courses and to help yellow jaundice'. The leaves of the white beet were used as spinach and added to *porrays* – a thick vegetable soup – and the roots, rich in sugar, were also a valuable food source. Boil red beets in salted water for 2-3 hours, beetroot is generally eaten cold – either freshly cooked or pickled in salads. Here's an old-fashioned recipe from *Mrs Beeton's Cookery* (1933):

Beetroot and Onion Salad
Use one part of thinly sliced onion and two parts of sliced picked beetroot.

Season with salt and pepper, moisten with vinegar and oil, and sprinkle with parsley.

History: Beets have been cultivated in England since Anglo-Saxon times and medieval cooks stuffed them into pies. Beetroot is often recorded as a popular dish in the Tudor era, while the Elizabethans enjoyed them in tarts and stews.

Magical use: Beetroot (*beta vulgaris*) was used in spells to attract love.

Cabbage

Cabbages were part of the staple diet in the Middle Ages and were small, loose-leaved plants of which Culpeper wrote: *'Cabbages are extremely windy whether you take them as meat or medicine...'* The leaves were used to treat inflammations and heal sores – a use that is equally valid today. For the small garden, red cabbage is the only variety worth considering as a vegetable, although some ornamental cabbages can be grown for their healing properties. Usually grown for pickling, red cabbage can be cooked with apple and served as an accompaniment for game. Here's another recipe from *Mrs Beeton's Cookery* (1933):

Pickled Red Cabbage
One good, firm red cabbage
1 quart of vinegar
Half an ounce of whole pepper
Half ounce of allspice

Remove the outer leaves; quarter the cabbage and remove the centre stalk. Cut each section across into very fine strips. Pile the shredded cabbage on a large plate and sprinkle it liberally with salt, and let it remain until the following day. Meanwhile boil the vinegar, pepper and spice together; strain and allow to go cold.

Drain and place in glass before pouring on the vinegar. It will be ready to use in three or four days; if kept for any length of time it loses its crispness.

History: Although the evidence points to the eastern Mediterranean and Asia as the places of origin, Celtic knowledge of it was so ancient as to have influenced the Latin name, *brassica* (from the Celtic word *bresic*).

Magical use: Cabbage/kale (*brassica oleracea*) is used in spells to draw good luck. Turnip (*brassica rapa*) is used for protection and for spells to end a relationship. Black mustard (*brassica nigra*) is used in spells for protection, to increase fertility and to strengthen mental powers.

Carrots

These have both medicinal and culinary uses, growing best in light, well-drained soil in a sunny position, or one with minimal shade. Fresh young carrots can be served with melted butter and sprinkled with parsley, or eaten raw in salads, with dips or as a garnish. Larger, older carrots can be used in stews and casseroles, or mashed with swede, butter and black pepper for a warming winter vegetable. This recipe was taken from the famous French *Larousse Gastronomique* 1938.

> **Carrots in Béchamel Sauce**
> Whole baby carrots
> One pint of water
> Salt to taste
> One tablespoon sugar
> 4 tablespoons of butter
> Two tablespoons of béchamel sauce

Put the vegetables in a pan with the cold water and add the salt, sugar and butter. Bring to the boil and reduce the heat;

cover the pan and simmer until the liquid has practically evaporated. Drain and add the béchamel sauce before serving.

History: It is believed that the carrot originated some 5,000 years ago in Asia and slowly spread into the Mediterranean area. The vegetable was known to the Egyptians, Greeks and Romans, but not cultivated in England until medieval times.

Magical use: Wild carrots (*daucus carota*) were used in spells to increase fertility and lust.

Peas

Peas have been cultivated in Britain since Roman times and used in soups, pottages and many other dishes. Dried they provided food for the winter, and were also used to fatten domestic pigs and pigeons. They had various medicinal uses and the water in which peas have been boiled was said to cure measles. Unfortunately, they are among the most difficult vegetables to grow, but are one of the most rewarding since the flavour of freshly picked peas is one of the greatest delicacies of the vegetable garden when served with a pat of butter.

Spring Peas and Pearl Onions
2 cups pearl onions
Salt
3 lb fresh shelled peas (about 4 cups)
¼ cup heavy cream
1 tbsp unsalted butter

Cream and butter make this old-fashioned side dish a family favourite. Use only fresh peas, cooked until they are just tender, for the very best flavour. Peel the onions by dropping them into boiling water for 1 minute, then slip off skins with a paring knife. Place in a heavy saucepan with half a cup of salted water. Cover and simmer over low heat for 20 minutes.

Add the peas and continue cooking for 5 minutes. Drain, return to the pan, and add cream and butter.

Heat through and serve.

History: The Greeks and Romans grew peas and during the Middle Ages they were an important part of the diet of ordinary people in Europe.

Magical use: None found.

Nowadays it is possible to grow your own vegetables and the first step is to pick up a selection of gardening books that specialise in small gardens from your local library. A few hours planning may reap rewards when setting up a true wise woman's vegetable plot to integrate with herbs and flowers as part of traditional wort-lore.

Chapter Two

The Goodwife

'To connect with the divine a witch will step outside, take a cup of coffee and sit in the garden, to be outside with nature... A Kitchen Witch will also get that connection in the kitchen, working with herbs, spices, plants and produce. Everything a Kitchen Witch makes is made with love, affection and a little bit of magic,' writes Rachel Patterson in *Pagan Portals: Kitchen Witchcraft*. For the parish pump witch, wise woman and cunning folk, the kitchen acted as consulting room, dispensary and temple, and as Rachel Patterson adds: 'A Kitchen Witch will create...recipes, crafts, lotions and potions. When a friend is poorly a Kitchen Witch will work a spell to aid, but will also make some homemade soup, putting healing energy into making it, adding healing energy with each vegetable and herb that is added.'

Incidentally, 'Goodwife' is an archaic title of respect where the woman addressed was of a lesser social rank than someone who was mistress of a household. The term was used in England, Scotland, and Colonial America, with the earliest known use given as circa 1325; by the mid-18th century it was outdated although it was a title often given to local wise women and cunning-women, in addition to being used as a form of address by Arthur Miller in his historical fiction *The Crucible*.

Larder and Kitchen

When food or money was scarce (especially during the war years) every scrap would have been eked out to last. Today we throw away seven million tonnes of food and drink every year, and more than half of this is could have eaten. In the USA more than twenty pounds weight of food per person per month is thrown away. The foods most wasted are fresh vegetables and salad, drink, fresh fruit, and bakery items such as bread and cakes; and there are two main reasons why good food is thrown away: we cook or prepare too much or don't use it in time.

Some modern wise women are fortunate that some of those economical war-time hints and recipes have been passed on as part of a family tradition. Many can still come in handy when there's still a week to go before the salary is paid into the bank, and everyone has been in that situation at sometime in their lives. Even the original domestic goddess, Mrs Beeton (1933 edition), had something to say on the subject in what she called 'the Art of 'Using Up'': 'Great care should be taken that nothing which might, by proper management, be turned to good account is thrown away, or suffered to be wasted in the kitchen.'

The key-word here is, of course – 'management' – managing food is the clever way to save those pennies, and often pounds. With just a little bit of thought, it is easy to create some delicious meals from leftovers – and that doesn't have to mean 'boring'. Unfortunately, we live in an age where frugality is viewed as a vice rather than a virtue, but never mind what the rest of the family thinks – don't discard *any* left-over food, put it in a plastic container and freeze it. Saving food lessens the adverse environmental impact on the planet and that's what *The Secret People* are all about!

For example, it's amazing how many meals you can get from one chicken! If you enjoy a roast on Sunday, the remains would make a great curry or a delicious risotto later in the week, and you'll always find enough for a sandwich. After that, the carcass can be boiled for stock and soups; which is a cue for the ultimate, classic comfort food for anyone under the weather – Jewish penicillin, the feel-better chicken soup. There are as many different recipes as there are Jewish grandmothers, but it's something that should go in everyone's cook book.

Like a lot of things that are consigned to folklore, old wives' tales and rural customs, there *is* more than a grain of truth behind the claims that chicken soup lessens the sniffles and acts as a pick-me-up. A study conducted by the American College of Chest Physicians found that chicken soup could help reduce upper-respiratory inflammation, which leads to those annoying symptoms of a cold, like a stuffy head and incessant sneezing. They found this particular old wives' tale exists in many cultures and that grandma's chicken soup is prescribed around the world because it really does make people feel better. Researchers first tested a recipe that was passed down from a Jewish team member's Lithuanian grandmother, containing chicken, onions, sweet potatoes, parsnips, turnips, carrots, celery, parsley, salt and pepper, and found the soup did have an anti-inflammatory effect. The researchers then tested a variety of canned chicken soups and found that store-bought versions could be just as effective.

Standard Recipe for Chicken Soup
Chicken carcass
Onions
Sweet Potatoes
Parsnips
Turnips
Carrots
Celery
Parsley
Salt and pepper

Peel the vegetables and cut into good sized chunks. Put all the ingredients into a pot with water and bring to a rapid boil. Skim the surface and remove all floating scum. Turn it down to a very low heat and simmer for two hours because the longer it simmers, the better the soup will be. Let the soup cool and refrigerate overnight. Any fat will rise to the surface and harden and make it easy to remove. Scoop off the fat and bring the soup back to the boil. Simmer until it's time to serve.

Here is scientific endorsement that this little bit of kitchen-Craft really works and should be in everyone's repertoire of healing – and every bit of goodness in the chicken is used. For a change, boil the chicken with just an onion and carrot and add tinned or frozen sweetcorn to the soup before serving.

The Art of 'Using Up'

- If you have any dinner left, box it and pop it in the freezer as a 'ready meal' for one. Even the smallest amount could be pureed up for a baby, or served as a kid's portion for lunch the next day.
- Keep trimmed bacon fat for frying and any bones or left-over meat should be used for making into stock for soups or gravy.
- Cold sausages can be sliced and added to potato salad or mash; or seasoned and used for fillings for sandwiches or jacket potatoes.
- Ends of cheese can be grated and mixed with equal amounts of fresh cheese to use in cooked dishes such as Welsh rarebit and jacket potatoes.
- Crusts and stale bread can be blitzed in the food processor to make breadcrumbs, which can be stored in the freezer. The same can be done with cake or biscuits and used as a topping for crumbles and puddings.
- Use slices of stale bread in a bread and butter pudding or to make 'eggy bread' by beating an egg in a bowl with seasoning. Cut slices of bread in half then dip in the egg and fry.
- The last dregs of wine or beer can be frozen in ice cube trays and popped out into stews and casseroles when cooking.
- Cut the bruises off old apples and toss into the pan with

your sausages. Don't throw out those black bananas – mash them up and add cream for a super-quick pudding.

Just because funds are limited doesn't mean that *The Secret People* must go without a few luxuries. Why not use an old charm for 'money drawing' that simply requires a purse or wallet being turned over at the new moon (see Chapter Six: The Fortune-Teller – Spell Casting), but while waiting for it to work, consider some of the delicacies that appealed to our forebears. After all, Charles I had a favourite dish of fried violet leaves, served with honey and sugar; not to mention the 17th century recipe that recommended primrose and cowslip flowers be used as flavouring for minnows fried with egg yolk! Or...

Marigold Pudding [1699]
Take a pretty quantity of marigold flowers very well shred, mingle with a pint of cream on new milk and almost a pound of good beef suet chopt very smalle, the gratings of a twopenny loaf and stirring all together put it into a bag flower'd and tie it fast. It will be boiled within an hour – or bake it in a pan.

Honey, Salt and Vinegar
No self-respecting parish pump witch, cunning or wise woman would be caught without honey, salt and vinegar in her kitchen. These three ingredients form an important part of healing and protection, as well as enhancing the flavour of cooking. They can also be used to treat minor ailments (see Chapter Three: The Parish Healer – Medicine Cupboard) such as sore throats, mouth problems and skin treatments, while honey is now believed to combat certain types of cancer.

Honey
Few people are fortunate enough to keep bees, but good honey is now widely available from farmers' markets, health shops and

delicatessens. Honey is the oldest known method of sweetening food and was used extensively in cooking and preserving long before cane sugar came to be widely used in the West. The Bible and the Koran contain mentions of honey; it was used in ancient Egypt for embalming, in India for preserving food, and has long been famed for its medicinal properties. The flavour of the honey depends on the flowers from which the bees take the nectar; clover, rosemary and heather are among the most prized, and honey from Mount Hymettus in Greece is particularly famous. Clear honey should be used in cooking, but for medicinal uses and the sheer pleasure of spreading on thick buttered toast, keep a jar of the thick crystallised honey in store.

Salt

There are many customs and superstitions relating to salt and few people will be unaware of the claim that bad luck will fall on anyone who, after spilling some, does not take a pinch and throw it over their left shoulder. Although the ritual is familiar throughout the world, its origins are obscure and it seems most likely to have begun because salt was regarded by the ancients as a sacred and precious commodity. Salt has received a bad press in recent years having been listed as a health hazard, but for the parish-pump witch, and her wise woman and cunning-woman counterparts, it is still a vital ingredient for spell casting.

Salt is the symbol for Elemental North/Earth and most make do with the common table variety. There is, however, an alternative that is much purer and native to these shores – Maldon Salt. This unmistakeable brand of flaky sea salt has been produced on the banks of the Blackwater Estuary for the past 130 years and has been gathered there since Roman times. The salt is 'harvested' according to the elements and the best time for drawing off the salted water from the estuary is during the high spring tides that occur twice a month – one just before the full moon and one just before the new moon. This is when the saline content of the water is at its highest since it has absorbed all the salt drying on the marsh grass. A heavy rainfall during the preceding week means that the freshwater content will be too high to produce good quality salt and so production is halted until the weather improves and the tide is right.

Consecrated Salt

Use Maldon Salt magically to represent the Element of Earth. Hold both hands cupped together, palms facing downwards over the small bowl containing the salt and visualise energy flowing from the palms into the salt. Pause for a moment and feel the power making the salt glow and becoming 'magically alive'. From now on this salt is a highly charged magical substance and should be kept solely for magical use. To make consecrated water use one teaspoon of Maldon Salt to a small bowl of water and repeat the above rite; use for blessing, cleansing and protective charms.

Taking Bread and Salt

This is a traditional acceptance that once having taken 'bread and salt' under someone's roof, the guest is honour-bound not to harm them for any reason. Although many traditional witches still observe this custom, it has now fallen into disuse – but be wary of anyone coming into your home who will accept neither food nor drink. Similarly, if in the company of an enemy it is important to ensure that no food or drink is accepted from that hand as this act is equally binding.

Vinegar

From the Bible to Cleopatra, to the samurai warriors of Japan, vinegar has been documented as a powerful liquid that ensures strength, power and long life. It was first mentioned for its preservation and healing powers about 7,000 years ago in Babylon; its production was a substantial industry from the 17th century in England and by the early 19th century flavoured vinegars were becoming popular in cooking. Vinegar (especially cider vinegar) contains health-giving properties helping to fight off infections, cleanse the blood and cure insomnia. As a household cleaner, vinegar is better than most commercial cleansers because it does not have any harsh, abrasive effects.

Preserves, Chutney and Pickles

It's quite easy to make good preserves, chutney and pickles if using fresh and slightly under-ripe, rather than over-ripe fruit and vegetables. With the increase of convenience foods many of the old kitchen skills have fallen from favour. Nevertheless, there is still a tremendous satisfaction in seeing a well-stocked larder of homemade produce waiting to be enjoyed out of season. There is also the added advantage of having something home-made to include in ritual celebrations as a true offering to the gods of the household.

For example, quinces (japonica apples) can be made into an unusual accompaniment to roast and cold meats, and cheese. The tree is grown for its ornamental appeal with lovely pink blossom in the spring, but the fruit is usually allowed to fall; keep an eye open for friends and neighbours who have a japonica bush growing on the side of their house! Although the fruit is not eaten raw because of its astringent flavour and the hardness of its flesh, it was cooked in pies and tarts with apples, pumpkin or marrow. Cultivated for more than 3,000 years, the tree with its beautiful blossom was probably introduced into northern Europe by the Romans. The fruit contains a large amount of pectin that makes it ideal for use in jams, jellies, marmalade, syrups, preserves and home-made wines. Culpeper cites its medicinal uses, but it does not appear to have any magical purpose.

Quince Jelly
Quinces
Sugar
Water

Wipe the fruit carefully; do not peel, but cut into quarters and put in a preserving pan with sufficient cold water to cover. Bring slowly to the boil and simmer gently until the fruits are tender. Strain through muslin but do not squeeze or the jelly will not be clear. Add 1lb sugar to each pint of juice and boil until setting point is reached. Pour into warm jars and allow to cool before sealing.

Nothing can beat the taste of home-made pickled onions to serve with cold meats and cheese. This tried and tested recipe was adapted from *Mrs Beeton's Every Day Cookery & Housekeeping Book* (1872 edition).

Pickled Onions
Choose small shallots (scallions) so as many as possible will fit into a large Kilner jar. Fill the jar with peeled onions and cover with cold vinegar. For extra bite use malt vinegar and a table-spoon of pickling spice. Seal the jar with an air-tight rubber ring and store for 2-3 months before eating; consume within 6-8 moths while the onions are still crisp.

Another simple family recipe uses apples for chutney that goes well with everything.

Grandmother's Apple Chutney
¾ lb brown sugar
1 lb cooking apples
¾ lb raisins
¾ lb onions

1 teaspoon ginger
1 teaspoon cayenne pepper
1 tablespoon salt
1 pint vinegar

Peel and core the apples; put them with the raisins and onion through a mincer. Mix the vinegar and sugar in a saucepan and bring to the boil; add all the other ingredients and bring back to the boil. Simmer for 20-30 minutes, stirring all the time. Put it into warm jars and allow to cool before sealing.

Warnings
- Do not allow anything metallic to come into contact with pickles or vinegar.
- Do not attempt to prepare any type of pickles during menstruation as this will 'turn' the vinegar sour. This can also apply to wine-making, so rather than run the risk of spoiling the produce, wait for a few days.

Once preserving has become part of the kitchen witch's year, it is possible to experiment with all manner of different recipes – both new and old. And another handy hint: when money is scarce a selection of attractively packaged preserves make a nice birthday or Yuletide gift for a friend.

View your kitchen as a special place to be; somewhere where you can create all manner of wonders from Nature's bounty of the garden, the farmers' market or the hedgerow.

Bask in the magical colours radiating from those glass jars stacked on the shelves in the larder.

Stillroom

These days supermarkets provide 'seasonal' foods all year round and it is easy to forget that only fifty years ago all produce was only available at certain times of the year. In former times preserving herbs and flowers was as much part of good house-keeping as was preserving fruit and berries and making home-made wine. The preservation of herbs and flowers was so important that country houses had a special room known as the 'stillroom' where these were prepared and preserved in many different ways, including the distilling of fragrant waters, and it was this 'still' that gave the room its name. *The Secret People*, of course, didn't have the luxury of a purpose-built room and so they had to improvise. The following, taken from an apothecary's notebook, was used during the 19th century:

Simple Distilling of Waters from Herbs and Flowers

Tie a piece of muslin or gauze over a glazed earthen pot, whose mouth is just large enough to receive the bottom of a warming pan. On this cloth lay your [fresh] herb chopped (mint, lavender, etc.,) then place upon them the hot warming pan with live coals in it, to cause enough heat just to prevent burning, by which means, as the steam issuing out of the herb cannot mount upwards, by reason of the bottom of the pan just fitting the brim of the vessel below it, it must necessarily descend, and collect into water at the bottom of the receiver, and that strongly impregnated with the essential oil this distilled.

When you want to make spirits or compound water it is easily done by simply adding some good spirits (i.e. strong distilled alcohol, vodka works well), or add French brandy to it, which will keep good for a long time. Care should be taken not to let the fire be too strong (least the herbs scorch), and to be made of charcoal for continuance and better regulation, which must be managed by lifting up and laying down the lid to increase or decrease the heat. The deeper the earthen pot, the cooler the steam; and the less fire at first (afterwards to be gradually raised) in the greater perfection will the distilled water be obtained.

[*A Witch's Treasury for Hearth & Garden*, Gabrielle Sidonie]

To bring this method up to date, the modern wise woman could use a Pyrex saucepan since these are heat-proof; a clear one will reveal what is going on inside and make sure the leaves don't scorch. A metal plate, or an all-metal pan lid (not with a plastic knob – it will melt!) can be used as a chaffing dish to provide the heat over the top. Leave the dish covered to cool down naturally.

The Woman's Treasury for Home & Garden gave instructions for the preparation of a lavender cordial said to relieve hysteria and nausea if a few drops were taken on a lump of sugar. The recipe is possibly a forerunner of the now famous 'rescue remedy'. The following are simple recipes for the beginner to try and if they go wrong little has been wasted.

Aunt Selina's Red Lavender Drops
The [lavender] blossoms have to be shredded into a small quantity of brandy. The liquid is then strained off a fortnight later, into small bottles and some ground cloves added.

Or another simple recipe:

Chamomile Aperitif
Add three tablespoons of chamomile flowers and 2oz sugar to a bottle of white wine. Store in a dark place for a month and shake each day. Strain and rebottle. Serve as an aperitif.

To serve as a digestive wine or liqueur after a meal:

Flower or Herb Cordial
Add four tablespoons of chopped rosemary to a bottle of white wine and leave to stand for two weeks. When ready to use, strain and rebottle. As an alternative, make as above and add hawthorn or pinks for a sweeter taste – hyssop or sage for a stronger flavour.

The following home-made fruit drinks make a pleasant alternative to shop-bought squashes and can be used as part of any ritual celebrations. Ideal for summer drinks in the garden.

Apple Water

Bake or roast some well-flavoured apples, place them in a pitcher and fill with boiling water. Strain off after a few hours and sweeten with honey before drinking.

Rowan Lemonade

The pretty rowan tree with its abundant red berries in autumn makes a lovely pink lemonade. Wash one cup of crushed, ripe berries and soak in three cups of cold water for one to two hours. Strain and add honey to taste. Pour into tall glasses over ice cubes and garnish with a few fresh berries. Makes a delightful and refreshing drink.

The pedantic reader may notice that the recipe doesn't actually contain any lemons, but back in the good old days details like that didn't count for much.

Traditional Lemonade

8 large lemons
8oz caster sugar
4 pints boiling water

Wash and dry the lemons. Remove the peel very carefully with a potato peeler; squeeze the lemon juice from the lemons and put in a covered container in the fridge or larder. Put the peel in a large bowl or jug with the sugar; pour over boiling water, stir briskly, cover and leave overnight in a cool place. Next day add the reserve lemon juice; strain into jugs and chill. Makes about 16 glasses.

This is a traditional recipe for old-fashioned lemonade and a refreshing drink for summer.

Home-Made Wines and Beer

Although home-brewing from commercial kits is a popular pastime, the annual production of wine from seasonal berries is a dying art. Good home-made wine is equal to fine brandy or port, and the garden produce of any mixed fruits, vegetables and flowers enables *The Secret People* to lay down an annual store of excellent wines. Some of the old recipes are so simple and yet the results are far superior to many wines in the supermarket for special occasions and celebrations.

Recipe for Blackberry Wine From a 19th Century Witch's Spell Book

1 gill blackberries
1 gill boiling water
3lbs sugar to each gallon of liquor
(or 4lbs if the wine is to be kept for some time)

Put the fruit into a deep vessel and pour on boiling water. When cool enough to handle, mash the berries with the hands, then cover and leave to stand until the pulp has risen and formed a crust (about three to four days). Strain and add sugar in the above proportions. Leave to work for seven to ten days. When finished working, bottle and cork tightly and keep for six months. **An excellent wine to use the following year at Spring Equinox or Beltaine**.

Note: Blackberries should not be picked after Old Michaelmas Day as it was believed the Devil had pissed on them. In truth the berries deteriorate late in the season and develop a kind of mould, which makes them unsuitable for eating.

Traditional Recipe for Damson Wine
1½ gallons boiling water
13lbs bruised damsons
Brown sugar

Pour boiling water on the bruised fruit. Stand for 48 hours and draw off the liquor. Add 2½lb sugar to every gallon of liquid. Place in a clean cask (container) and fill up. When it is half finished fermenting fill up again and cork tightly. Bottle after the wine has stood for nine months. Do not use until a year later as the wine improves by keeping.
An ideal libation to offer at Harvest Home or Winter Solstice.

Elderberry Liqueur
2lbs of elderberries
1 bottle of vodka
4oz sugar
Rind of half a lemon

Put the elderberries into large jar and add the lemon rind (with as little pith as humanly possible) and top up with vodka. Seal then shake the jar and it put into a dark cupboard for three months. Pour the sugar into a clean, empty bottle and strain the liquor over the top of it. Shake vigorously and return to the cupboard for at least two months, shaking once a week for the first week, then less. After this time it is perfectly drinkable but, if you can manage to restrain yourself, it will improve with age as long as it is left sealed.
Excellent for paying homage to the Ancestors or toasting in the Yule festivities.

Mulled Ale for Yule
1 quart of good ale

1 glass of rum or brandy
1 tablespoon caster sugar
Pinch ground cloves
Pinch grated nutmeg
Pinch ground ginger

Put the ale, sugar and spices into a pan and bring to boiling point. Add the brandy and more sugar and flavouring if necessary and serve at once. The traditional way of heating the ale was to plunge a red-hot poker in the pewter mug. **A perfect winter drink for Yule and the Winter Solstice.**

Elder Flower Wine
1 quart elder flowers
1 gallon cold water
4lbs sugar
3 sliced lemons
1 yeast cake or 10oz baker's yeast

Pick the stems from enough blossoms to fill a quart measure when crushed down. Add cold water and steep for 24 hours. Strain and add the sugar, sliced lemons and yeast cake. Cover and stand for two weeks. Strain carefully and pour into a crock or container. Cover and bottle after five months. **An ideal libation for the Summer Solstice or Lammas.**

Dandelion Beer
3 quarts dandelion petals
2 lemons
½ or whole ginger
1 gallon water
Slice of toast spread with yeast

Put the dandelion petals in a cask or container. Bring the water to boiling point and leave to cool. When tepid, pour over the petals. Cover with a cloth and leave for three days, stirring daily. Strain off and add the rinds of lemons, crushed ginger and sugar. Boil for 30 minutes; add the strained lemon juice and the piece of toast spread with yeast. Skim the next day. Put in a cask and leave for seven weeks before bottling.

An ideal home-made libation to offer for the Midsummer or Lammas celebrations.

Traditional Sloe Gin

After the first frost, half fill clean, dry wine bottles with the fruit previously pricked with a darning needle. Add to each bottle 1oz crushed barley-sugar (or 4oz brown sugar). Fill the bottles with dry, unsweetened gin, cork them securely, and allow them to remain in a moderately warm place for three months, turning weekly. At the end of this time strain the liqueur through fine muslin until quite clear, then bottle. Cork securely and store away in a cool, dry place until required for use. This can be used as an alternative to commercially prepared 'rescue remedies'.

Made from the fruit of the blackthorn, this liqueur certainly has 'Otherworldly' qualities and would be perfect for Samahin/Hallowe'en.

Honey Beer for Harvest

1 cup hops
8oz honey or sugar
1 gallon water
1 teaspoon granulated yeast (or 1 tablespoon fresh baker's yeast)

Boil the hops and honey (or sugar) for one hour in a large pan with as much of the water as possible. Strain into a plastic bucket and make up to one gallon with cold water. Allow it to cool. Add granulated yeast or float a slice of toast spread with brewer's yeast. Cover loosely and leave in a warm place for 48 hours. Siphon it off without disturbing the yeast deposit into one gallon jars or flagons and cork. Stand it in a cool place for a week when it will be ready to drink. Tie the corks down if keeping longer than a week and although this is a quickly made, thirst-quenching drink, it should not be kept for long. **An ideal drink to prepare for Lammas or the Autumn Equinox.**

Negus or Mulled Claret

1 pint claret
½ pint boiling water
Sugar, nutmeg and cinnamon to taste

Heat the claret nearly to boiling point and add the boiling water, sugar, nutmeg and cinnamon, and serve hot. Any kind of wine may be mulled, but port and claret are those usually selected.
An excellent warming drink for any of the Fire Festivals.

Wassail for Twelfth Night

6 cooking apples
Soft brown sugar
½oz ground ginger
½oz grated nutmeg
Pinch of powdered cinnamon
8oz Demerara sugar
3 pints mild or brown ale
½ bottle of raisin wine
¼ bottle of sherry
1 lemon
Lump sugar

Core the apples but do not peel them. Fill the holes with soft brown sugar and roast in a moderate oven for 45 minutes to 1 hour, taking care they do not burst. Mix together in a saucepan the ginger, nutmeg, cinnamon and Demerara sugar; add one pint of ale and bring to the boil. Stir in the rest of the ale, wine, sherry, and ten lumps of sugar that have been rubbed on the rind of the lemon. Heat the mixture, but do not allow it to boil this time. Put the roasted apples in a large punch bowl and pour in the hot ale mixture with half the peeled and sliced lemon.

Traditionally prepared to toast the apple trees on Twelfth Night to ensure a bumper harvest in the coming year.

It is a fallacy to think that wine cannot be made in small quantities; it is possible to turn out six or less bottles at a brewing. Small quantities can be made without a lot of equipment – the wine, after straining can be put straight into the bottles from the fermenting bowl, and the bottles left covered until the fermentation stops, when they can be corked. These special brews can then be kept for those important ritual occasions.

Household Hints

Most people have memories of the things their grandmothers used to correct minor domestic mishaps, and most of those memories are evoked by smells: iodine, Friar's Balsam, carbolic soap, paraffin oil, beeswax. While few understood the science behind the various different remedies, they were resurrected each time there was something to be cleaned, repelled or rejuvenated. Here are some examples:

Insect Repellents

From the earliest times, herbs have been hung in the home to repel insects and six drops of rosemary oil mixed with a pint of water can be used as an effective insect-repellent spray. Most insects avoid feverfew and bunches hanging to dry in the kitchen will keep them away; sage has much the same effect on flies. For other insects try:

- Ants: Pennyroyal, peppermint.
- Fleas: Alder leaves, winter savoury, pennyroyal.
- Moths: Spearmint, thyme, woodruff, pennyroyal, camphor, cedar, lavender, rue, chamomile, pyrethrum, winter savoury.

When cottages and great baronial halls still scattered reeds on the stones floors, 'strewing herbs' were included to cover offensive smells because the scent was released when they were walked on. During the Middle Ages bay and tansy were used as strewing herbs, valued not only for the scent, but also as an insect repellent; fennel was used as a strewing herb in medieval monasteries and churches. Lavender was multi-purpose in that it was used as a strewing herb, insect-repellent and a mask for unpleasant smells; while the 'fume of smoke' from rosebay willowherb was said to drive away flies and gnats.

In medieval times toads were often kept as pets in the pantry to get rid of flies and other unwanted visitors, which was probably what led to the creature being identified as witches' familiars. Up until Victorian times, gardeners continued to encourage toads to live in the big greenhouses for exactly the same purpose.

Mirrors

One of the most enduring superstitions and still a most widely spread belief is that seven years' bad luck will follow the breaking of a mirror. This probably stems from the belief that a mirror reflects the soul and if the image was shattered, the soul would be in mortal danger – or that it took seven years for a replacement to be bought! An old English custom following the accidental breakage was to carefully collect all the pieces together and take them to a river or fast running stream and hurl them in to avoid bad luck. Not an ecologically sound practice in view of the potential damage to wildlife!

There are many superstitions linking mirrors with death, but this may have referred to the fact that they were often seen as gateways to Otherworld and therefore to be avoided. Those who use mirrors for scrying or divination should keep the surface covered at all times and away from curious eyes. Similarly, mirrors used around the home should not be used for magical purposes. Old superstitions often have a root of truth in their words.

The best way to clean mirrors without streaks is to do so with a mixture of vinegar and water. This simple method is extremely effective and when wiped away with crumpled newspaper, you avoid the lint left behind by paper towels and cloths.

Copper, Bronze, Pewter and Brass
Items discovered at car boot sales (yard sales) are often treasures that are suitable for magical or ritual working, but they must be thoroughly cleansed before use. Two 'natural' cleaning agents for brass and copper are:

- Removing corrosion spots with vinegar or lemon juice mixed with salt.
- A polish made using equal parts vinegar and tomato ketchup.

Burnt copper saucepans should never be scoured or filled with soda water; although it removes all the burnt particles, it makes the saucepans liable to burn again. Fill them with salt and water and leave until the next day, then bring slowly to boiling point. The burnt particles should come off without any difficulty, and there will be no after-effects.

Warning: Copper vessels used for any purposes connected with the preparation of food, should be kept scrupulously clean and dry because any damp and dirt that remains may produce 'poisonous salts on the metal'. Fruits and vegetables should not be prepared in copper pans.

Also beware of using old pewter for food and drink because old pewter contains lead, which over time can escape from the vessel and become a health hazard. Sometimes it takes years to develop symptoms and damage is likely being caused to your organs during that time. If ingesting lead in small amounts then the amount of lead in the body can continue to increase until acute lead poisoning is fatal. Since 1910, however, tabletop pewter has not contained lead making it safe to eat and drink from and as for cleaning...dampen cabbage leaves with vinegar, dip the leaves in salt and use them to scrub the pewter clean. Rinse with water and a gentle soap after that, followed by drying with a soft cloth.

Bronze, however, should not be cleaned with any commercial preparation, but should be washed and continuously buffed with a clean cloth, since cleaning destroys the patina that gives bronze its appeal. For a more shiny look, place two tablespoons of baking soda in a small dish; drizzle a small amount of lemon juice onto the baking soda and mix until a soft paste forms. Apply the paste with a small polishing cloth using small circular motions. Allow the paste to stay on the item for 20 to 30 minutes then rinse thoroughly with warm water to remove the paste and buff dry with a clean towel.

Silver
Always clean tarnished silver next to an open window or in the open air because the fumes are sulphurous – and take care to cover stainless steel sinks as silver polish can leave unsightly marks. In an emergency, silver can be brightened by using a pad

soaked in white spirit – and it's best to wear a pair of cotton gloves during the process as the natural acid from the skin can actually tarnish silver.

Silver Cutlery

There is a superstition attached to cutlery that is quoted in many rural areas: *'Knife falls – gentleman calls; fork falls – lady calls; spoon falls – baby squalls.'* It is also unlucky to cross two knives at table as this indicates hostile intent. This practice of setting knives and forks carefully side by side on the table is said to be a throwback to the times when the knife was used for more than eating and to set it down beside the platter showed that the owner harboured no ill intent to anyone at his table. Anyone given a knife as a gift should immediately give the gift-bearer a small coin to ensure no bad luck strikes.

To clean silver cutlery, place a few items at a time in boiling water together with a heaped tablespoon of baking soda and pieces of tin foil (those old silver foil milk bottle tops were ideal). Soak for two minutes and remove, rinsing immediately with boiling water. Dry and polish with a clean cloth. For badly tarnished silver the process may need to be repeated.

Old Glassware

Old fashioned glassware is usually handed down in the family but can be obtained at car boot sales and has multiple uses. Unfortunately cheap glass has a tendency to cloud over with a white film, but this can usually be removed with vinegar, baking soda, or even lemons. Scrubbing the glass with toothpaste can also remove the film.

To loosen glass stoppers, pour a little olive oil around the stopper and place the bottle or decanter near the fire, then tap the stopper lightly. The warmth will cause the oil to seep around and loosen the stopper.

To remove stains from the bottom of glass decanters, tear

newspaper into small pieces and drop into the bottom. Mix a tablespoon of bicarbonate of soda in warm water and pour into the decanter. Allow it to stand for a few minutes and then shake vigorously. Repeat the process until the marks disappear.

On Candles and Wax

To make candles burn well yet last longer, first light the wick and allow it to burn until a small pool of melted wax forms, then (without burning yourself) take a little salt and sprinkle it around the wick. For candles that have become bent (not snapped), immerse them in a bowl of warm water for a minute or two then gently ease them back into shape.

Old, forgotten candles found lurking at the bottom of a box or drawer are usually scratched, rough and coated with fluff and dust: To spruce them up simply hold the candle by its wick under hot running water, turning it until the outer layer of dirt and wax washes away, leaving a clean, new looking candle. It's advisable to run plenty of boiling water down the sink afterwards to ensure the wax doesn't block the pipe, or else collect the run-off water in a bowl and let it cool. Once cold, the solidified wax drips can be safely discarded or recycled.

In *Pagan Portals: Candle Magic*, Lucya Starza suggests a practical method of recycling candles:

Gather up all your candle stubs and bits of wax clinging to candle holders, plus a container that once held a candle. You will need to buy a new pre-stiffened wick with a small metal disc at the bottom (a sustainer). The old wax will need to be melted. Don't put it into a pan that goes straight onto the cooker, use a double-boiler or place a basin inside a pan of boiling water. If your wax was previously part of a spell candle, to dispel the old magic stir it three times widdershins while it is melting and say: '*I dispel all influences on this wax. Be gone, be gone, be gone.*' When the wax has all melted, dip the end of the wick with the sustainer into the wax just to coat it, then pop it into the container and let the wax stick it to the bottom. Then carefully pour the rest of the melted wax in around the wick. If it is a tall container you will need to place a pencil or something across the top and prop the wick against it to stop it from listing to one side. Leave the candle somewhere to cool down and set – the fridge is ideal. Trim the wick to a centimetre or two before lighting the candle.

Using candles invariably results in wax being spilled onto surfaces and materials, so here are a few simple tips on how to deal with it. On robes and altar cloths simply place a sheet of clean brown paper over the wax and press gently with a cool iron. Keep moving the paper around to a clean patch until no more grease comes up under the iron and the marks are removed completely.

This method works equally well on carpets and rugs, but just be sure to use a sheet of paper large enough to ensure the iron doesn't make direct contact with the carpet as many man-made fibres melt easily! For small spills, an old brown envelope opened out will do nicely, but avoid the adhesive. Before switching the iron off it is a good idea to turn up the heat and iron an old tea towel to ensure the plate is spotless, otherwise grease may be transferred to clothes or linen.

For polished wooden surfaces, a good method is to place a sheet of polythene (a plastic carrier bag will do) over the wax, then place something out of the freezer on top for a couple of minutes to thoroughly chill the wax. This should now be easily removed with a thumbnail or a very blunt knife – such as a butter knife. The wax should flick off, often in one piece.

Recipe for Home-made Furniture Polish
4oz beeswax
1 pint turpentine

1 pint water
2oz white wax
1oz hard soap
½oz lavender oil

Put the hard soap and water into an old pan and heat until the soap is dissolved; heat the beeswax and white wax in a tin in the oven until they melt. Mix together while hot then carefully add the turpentine and lavender oil (away from any naked flame). Bottle and shake well every day until the mixture thickens – then after about 14 days it will be ready to use. It's a nice idea to make this up and keep it solely for magical or ritual use, e.g. wooden platter, candlesticks, wand, staff or thumb-stick, and knife handles. Not only does the polish give a beautiful finish to things, it also imparts a lovely old-fashioned smell.

Nature's Neutraliser
One of the most powerful non-commercial cleaners is good, old-fashioned baking soda (or bicarbonate of soda). For example:

Clean the Microwave: Baking soda on a clean damp sponge cleans gently inside and outside the microwave and never leaves a harsh chemical smell. Rinse well with water.

Clean Coffee and Tea Pots: Remove coffee and tea stains and eliminate bitter off-tastes by washing mugs and coffee makers in a solution of ¼ cup baking soda in 1 quart of warm water. For stubborn stains, try soaking overnight in the baking soda solution and detergent or scrubbing with baking soda on a clean damp sponge.

Keep Refrigerators Fresh: Place an open box in the back of the fridge to neutralize odours.

Deodorize the Cutting Board: Sprinkle the cutting board with baking soda, scrub, rinse.

Deodorize Lunch Boxes and Flasks: Between uses, place a tablespoon of dry baking soda in each flask and lunch box to absorb lingering odours, rinse and dry before use.

If family treasures and ritual objects can be kept looking bright and clean, there is no reluctance to use them. Also keep a look out for old cookery books and treasuries in second-hand book shops in order to build up a personal collection of traditional recipes and household hints.

The Linen Cupboard

With all the conveniences in the modern home there is no longer a need for the linen cupboard, but even with this reduced to a small 'airing' cupboard that usually houses a hot water tank, it is still possible to keep linen and towels in the old fashioned way by slipping a few sprigs of lavender between the folds. Since medieval times lavender was made into sachets for freshening and keeping moths away from linen, so *The Secret People* are merely carrying on this tradition.

Make muslin bags about four inches square and fill with *pot pourri* mixture to hang in clothes cupboards and drawers. Fill muslin bags with dried lavender flowers and leaves, and use in the same way to deter moths. Don't be tempted to recharge the contents with essential oil as this will seep through and stain the clothes or linen.

The Guest Room

Keep some sprays of lavender or small lavender bags to put under the pillow in the guest room so that the linen is perfumed. Lavender scented clothes hangers will also keep the wardrobe smelling sweet for guests. Gently spray lavender water onto the towels. Freshen closets by placing a box of baking soda on the shelf to keep the space smelling pleasant.

Scented Drawer Liners

Cut up patterned wallpaper into pieces of a suitable size; roll them up with thin sachets of *pot pourri* between the sheets. Wrap the whole in cling film and leave to mature for up to six weeks, then use the pieces to line your clothes and linen drawers.

Lavender Water for Ironing

A simple perfumed water can be made by putting a couple of drops of essential oil into a small bottle of distilled (or boiled) water. Shake well and the oil will be absorbed, giving a subtle perfume for fragrancing linen, handkerchiefs etc. This doesn't keep well and must be either used immediately or kept in the fridge. Put into a spray bottle and spray over linen while ironing, but **do not put into a steam iron**.

Herb Pillows

Herb pillows are very easy to create and can make all the difference between a restless night and a sound sleep. Different perfumes can affect the way we sleep and here are a couple of suggestions on how to utilise some of those home-grown herbs and flowers.

Sweet Dreams Pillow

Everyone knows that a sachet of hops beneath the pillow at night will encourage a good night's sleep, but other herbs can also be used to enhance sleep and encourage sweet dreams. In a large bowl mix together the following:

2 handfuls of hops
1 handful of basil
1 handful of chamomile

1 handful of lavender

Pour this blend into a large fabric sachet and seal. The fabric can be anything appropriate or appealing although white muslin is best because it has a loose, open weave that allows the perfume to escape easily. Whatever is used, make sure that there is a lot of room for the herbs to move about inside and also, so that when it is placed beneath a normal pillow, the sachet goes fairly flat and does not feel like a solid lump under the sleeper's head – or they will not get a very good night's sleep at all.

Prophetic Dreams Pillow
2 handfuls of hops
1 handful of mugwort
1 handful of chamomile
1 handful of aniseed

Do not use star anise as this is too strongly perfumed and the seed cases are hard and lumpy, which definitely will not help achieve your objective. Again mix the herbs beforehand in a large bowl and pour into the fabric sachet. For this one it is best to use something sumptuous like blue or purple velvet, but do make sure it is big enough to go almost flat when placed under the pillow.

If the objective is to dream about a future lover or spouse, add a handful of rose petals to the blend. The recipient should repeat a little phrase or rhyme when they go to bed that explains what the sleeper hopes to achieve. This should be repeated seven times before going to sleep. For example: *'As I lay me upon my bed/Show me who I am to wed.'*

Astral Travel Pillow
This one is not only to encourage the spirit to make astral

journeys, but also that the sleeper should remember the experience in the morning. According to some teaching, everyone travels/dreams every night, but very few remember anything about it – so the remembering is the important part. Take:

2 handfuls of hops
1 handful of rosemary
1 handful of aniseed
1 handful of elderflowers

Persistence and patience are key here. Every night before going to sleep, repeat the line: *'Tonight I will remember all my astral journeying.'* This must be carried out every night for one moon – 28 days – and after that (all being well), this should be accomplished at will.

Clean, sweet-smelling clothing and linen is a joy to use and commercially-prepared stain removers have made all the old fashioned methods obsolete. Nevertheless it is still one of life's little luxuries to make sure that even the most modest of 'airing cupboards' is lightly fragranced.

The Hearth Fire

The hearth is traditionally the centre of the home and, needless to say, there are many superstitions attached to this belief. The hearth fire is also the symbolic and magical centre of any witch's home, and it is to the hearth we bring the richness of Nature's bounty to help celebrate the old festivals and feast days. It is at the hearth fire we regularly use the four sacramental foods that have been part of spiritual observance since ancient times, oil (Elemental Fire), bread (Elemental Air), salt (Elemental Earth) and wine (Elemental Water).

Because the hearth fire was so important, it was thought to be unlucky for anyone other than a member of the family, or a long-standing friend, to poke the fire. If a fire that has been set catches light quickly and without any artificial aid, it was said that unexpected visitors would shortly arrive. If it draws badly, rain is expected; if it burns to one side, a wedding is in the offing; while one that crackles indicates frost. Once the fire is burning bright the well-being of absent family members or a loved one can be determined if the fire is poked and the shafts of flame leap upwards. If the fire roars up the chimney there will be an argument in the house, or a storm outside. Sparks at the back of the fireplace foretell important news on the way; and a fall of soot indicates ill-luck. An old English superstition says that flakes of soot hanging from the bars of a fire grate tell that a stranger will shortly be visiting the house; while if a volume of soot suddenly drops down the chimney there is money coming to one member of the family. It can also mean that bad weather is on the way – or that the chimney needs sweeping!

There is all manner of witch-lore attached to the hearth and *The Secret People* are conscious of the place the hearth fire plays in their lives – and should strive keep an open fire wherever possible. To honour the gods of the hearth make a regular offering – for example:

To Scent the House

If bay, lavender or rosemary is grown in the garden, burn the cuttings from pruning on the open fire. Or sprinkle a few drops of essential oil into the fire about 15 minutes before lighting.

As Eric Parker wrote in *The Countryman's Weekend Book*:

Of wood as a blessing in country places there is more to be said... Of wood fires in open hearths, of the ease and speed of lighting them, or the spirit and gaiety of their flame, of the gradual and thorough warmth they give to a room, of the happy sounds of their crackling twigs, of the beauty of the lighting and shadows cast by their flickering, and of the faint, comforting scent they send through the house ...

And some woods are better for burning that others, as is reflected in this traditional country rhyme:

Beechwood fires are bright and clear
If the logs are kept a year
Chestnut only good they say
If for long it's laid away
Make a fire of elder tree
Death within your house will be
But ash new or ash old
Is fit for a Queen with a crown of gold

Birch and Fir logs burn too fast
Blaze up bright and do not last
It is by the Irish said
Hawthorn bakes the sweetest bread
Elmwood burns like churchyard mould
Even the very flames are cold
But ash green or ash brown
Is fit for a Queen with a golden crown

Poplar gives a bitter smoke
Fills your eyes and makes you choke
Apple wood will scent your room
With an incense-like perfume
Oaken logs, if dry and old
Keep away the winter's cold
But ash wet or ash dry
A king shall warm his slippers by.

Since medieval times, burning ash-wood was said to drive away evil spirits; while apple and cherry wood burnt indoors will perfume the whole house for a Beltaine fire. Smoke from burning yew leaves was supposed to repel gnats and mosquitoes, as well as rats and mice. Burning blackthorn wood banishes negative energy, while holly burns very hot and very quickly, but can be burned freshly cut. **On no account, however, must elder wood be burned on the hearth fire as misfortune is sure to follow.**

Chapter Three

The Parish Healer

Seeking medicinal healing from *The Secret People* was nothing new and neither were their skills a myth. For more than a thousand years, until the 18th century, an unbroken tradition of skilled healing was handed down in one Myddfai family. At the beginning of the 13th century they were urged to write it all down 'as a record of their skill, lest no one should be found with the requisite knowledge as they were' and so this information can be studied in detail today. The Physicians of Myddfai were holistic in their approach, looking for the causes of a disease as well as attempting to alleviate its symptoms.

As Barbara Griggs comments in *Green Pharmacy: A History of Herbal Medicine*:

Myddfai use of medicinal herbs was obviously based on repeated observation in practice. They specified parts of the herb and quantity where they felt this was necessary, and were fussy about the cleanliness of the water used in their preparations. Like the Anglo-Saxon leeches, the Myddfai physicians used herbs in plain country style, brewed up in infusions, or crushed and mixed with lard to make a poultice. As peasants do, they used them singly, although occasionally the combined one with two or three others. Although they drew on what had been estimated as a range of 175 herbs and must have needed specially cultivated supplies, the ones they used most often were the simples which grew freely in the countryside, or could be cultivated with ease in a peasant's plot...

Practical healing is also an aspect that can and does incorporate the likes of charms and such, and yet again it is one of those subjects that needs careful consideration. Although there are innumerable examples of charms and rituals associated with plant healing from Anglo-Saxon times onwards, these seem to be associated with the practice of healers rather than with home-remedies. It is highly likely that often women described as witches were innocent practitioners of herbal medicine; while others liked to cultivate the image of witchcraft in order to enhance their reputations. Writing in 1584, Reginald Scott observes in *Discoverie of Witchcraft* and is quoted by Keith Thomas in *Religion and the Decline of Magic*: 'It is indifferent to say in the English tongue, 'she is a witch' or 'she is a wise woman'' – a confusion that persisted up until the present day.

Needless to say, common sense must play a major part in any healing and many so-called healers cause more harm than good because not enough thought has been put into the actions. As Annie Wyse, author of *Rainbow Bridge,* pointed out, it would be good to think that healing was always good and never did any harm, but this just isn't so.

From the moral perspective, we must also weigh in the balance our right to interfere in other people's destiny. A case to consider is the 'healing' requested by a mother on behalf of her daughter-in-law who *couldn't* have a baby. When the right line of questioning was adopted, it transpired that her son and his wife didn't know anything about the request. The mother-in-law was resentful because the couple were happy pursuing their respective careers and did not want to be tied down with children, and she was desperate for grandchildren. In this case the pregnancy would have been unwanted and unasked for. The people who should have been consulted knew nothing of the intended magical healing to be carried out on their behalf. **To put no finer point on it: this would have been black magic!**

Most healers agree that they are merely channels for the energy that enables healing to occur and these channels need to have certain properties if they are to work well. We may produce a healing charm, spell or ritual, but unless the 'healer' ensures that they are not polluting or obstructing the energy flow, their good intentions might just produce the opposite result! To work healing magic, our energy channels need to be:

- Clear of obstructions.
- Big enough to carry the flow.
- Strong enough not to break under the pressure of the flow.
- Without bends or kinks to divert the flow.
- Going to the right place.
- Carrying the right stuff.
- Without any other 'additives' that will pollute the energy.

Annie Wyse used the analogy of drinking water being piped into our homes.

> The same principles apply to healing energy 'piped' into us through magical healing. If any of the above conditions affecting the channel are not fulfilled then we are not receiving clear unpolluted magical/healing. And as healers, we are not giving pure energy to the recipient. If we get polluted water through the tap then we may suffer diseases as a result, or any illness we already have may be exacerbated by the polluted water.

For example, unclean or ill-defined magical energy can *feed* a cancer instead of killing it.

> Before agreeing to undertake a magical operation on behalf of someone else, the healer must take the responsibility of ensuring his or her channel is unpolluted. We need to be sure we are up to the job; that our channel is strong enough; that we are channelling the appropriate energy for this person at

this time. Being a clear and unpolluted channel for energy for any magical operation requires self-honesty. Being honest with ourselves enables us to recognise when we are getting didactic, when we know best, when we have 'the answer', when we can 'fix it', 'cure it'! Blinkered vision is the death knell to any effective magical operation – and especially healing.

Medicine Chest

For our grandparents, the ability to make a remedy from local produce or kitchen ingredients was considered to be one of the basic skills of home-making. They knew their remedies worked even if they weren't able to explain why. Kitchen cupboards of today contain a wider range of leaves, stems, barks, roots, seeds, fruits, nuts and pulses, but the witch and wise woman will still have some very basic ingredients in her medicine chest. Most of these will be found in her store cupboard – salt, honey, vinegar, onions and lemon. Dozens of effective remedies can be prepared from these five items before needing to set foot in the herb garden.

'Simples' were cures that consisted of one ingredient, i.e. simple to prepare and administer and in *Herbal Simples Approved for Modern Uses of Cure* by William Thomas Fernie (1895), cited a 1620 observation made by a country parson, and no doubt referring to the skills of the local cunning-folk:

> In the knowledge of Simples, wherein the manifold wisdom of God is wonderful to be seen, one thing should be carefully observed, which is to know what herbs may be used instead of drugs of the same nature, and to make the garden the shop for home-bred medicines are both more easy for the Parson's purse, and more familiar for all men's bodies...

Salt: This has always been considered a precious commodity and apart from its culinary and magical properties, it has many uses in healing. Alchemists regarded salt as one of the three major elements alongside sulphur and mercury. A strong natural salt solution acts as an emetic and a purgative, while a very weak one can be applied to the skin as a cooling antiseptic and cleanser for wounds and mouths. A weak solution of salt water is one of the most effective gargles for treating a sore throat. A salt bath: one cup of sea salt can draw impurities through the skin – experience a 20-minute soak in a hot bath to feel the benefits after 'flu, or to treat tiredness and stiffness.

Honey: When used for medicinal purposes this should always be a single, unblended type, as this contains some of the qualities of the plants from which the bees have extracted the nectar. Honey is soothing, antiseptic, expectorant and healing. It can keep the blood thin, help balance blood pressure and improve circulation; it can be used to draw poisons or clean infected wounds. Honey and hot lemon juice is a soothing drink for those suffering from colds and 'flu.

Honey can quickly cure a hangover because it contains natural sugars, which are known to speed up the oxidation of alcohol by the liver and acts as a sobering agent. It is also really gentle on the stomach.

Granny's Honey Hangover Cure
1 tablespoon liquid honey
5 tablespoons orange juice
4 tablespoons natural yogurt

Blend all the ingredients together and enjoy the beneficial effects.

Herbal Cough Syrup
This recipe treats sore throats and tight chests. Thyme is a

good herb to use for a base for cough syrup and when made and stored correctly it should keep for a year.

1½oz chopped thyme
1½ pints water
1lb honey

Place the chopped herbs and the water into a pan and bring to the boil. Cover with a tight-fitting lid and reduce the heat to low, simmering gently for 20 minutes. Remove from the heat and set aside to cool with the lid still on the pan. Before straining into a jug or another pan, press the herbs down in the strainer with the back of a wooden spoon to extract all the goodness. Discard the squashed herbs and return the liquid to the heat, simmering gently without the lid until reduced to about a teacup full. Add the honey to the reduced liquid and stir over a low heat until it becomes a syrupy consistency. **Do not overheat or it will become herbal toffee.**
Pour into clean bottles when cool and label with name, date and dosage: Adults: 2-3 teaspoons 3-6 times daily. Child: 1 teaspoon 3-6 times daily.

Vinegar: This comes in many different guises and each has its own medicinal uses. It can be used for skin and hair preparation, washes and douches – use two teaspoons of vinegar to one cup of tepid water. A vinegar hair rinse keeps the scalp healthy and the hair in good condition. Diluted with cold or iced water, vinegar can be used to treat hot, swollen joints, or relieve tension headaches. Sage and vinegar were both traditionally used in compresses for easing sprains. Vinegar brings bruises to the surface, while it cools and reduces swelling – as quoted in the nursery rhyme 'Jack and Jill', where Jack 'went to bed to mend his head with vinegar and brown paper'. Many old rhymes for children contain snippets of old wisdom and it is a shame that these days fewer and fewer parents pass this on to young children. In fact, this was one simple way for the wise woman to pass on their knowledge – something that gets overlooked today. On a more modern note, the Yale-New Haven hospital used vinegar as a hospital disinfectant when after-surgery eye infections became a problem. They solved it by using vinegar because it is a powerful antiseptic and kills dangerous bacteria on contact.

To Treat Bruises

Apply a poultice of vinegar and brown paper. Put five or six sheets of strong brown paper in a pan of sage vinegar; put a lid on the pan and let it simmer on a low heat for a few minutes. A good quality paper should soften without breaking up. Remove from the heat and carefully remove the paper, wrapping it in over-lapping layers around the affected part. Use as hot as possible without burning the skin and build up several layers. Cover with cling film and bandage – not too tightly. Leave on for four hours. This poultice is very soothing and wonderfully supportive. Re-apply twice daily until the swelling and bruising subsides.

Onions: These can be used to treat wounds, spots, styes and ear infections; and can be used on young children and older people who don't like garlic – the 'remedy for all diseases and hurts' according to Culpeper. Onions can also be used as one of the most effective treatments for soothing chilblains. Cut a medium-sized onion in half, dip in a saucer of salt, and massage the chilblain with the onion gently but firmly to stimulate the circulation. Ideally get someone to do this for you and keep massaging for as long as possible as the massage relieves the burning sensation associated with chilblains, particularly those on the feet. Leeks contain similar properties, but in a milder form, while Welsh herbalists extol the virtues of leek soup to combat colds, coughs and pneumonia.

Lemons: Long used to treat a list of ailments. Lemon juice cleanses and tones the system and neutralises excess acidity in the body; and helps to relieve sluggishness of the liver and bowels. When taken with honey to relieve cold and 'flu symptoms, lemon acts as a cooling diuretic, lowering the temperature and helping the body to expel toxins. A glass of lemon juice every morning is a good way of maintaining a healthy system and warding off infections. It helps reduce high blood pressure, protect blood vessels and maintain tissue vitality, as well as alleviating rheumatism and gout. Externally, lemon juice can be used as an antiseptic for insect bites and chapped skin.

Preparation

The most common techniques for home-herbal preparation are infusions, decoctions, tinctures, poultices or compresses. Both fresh and dried herbs can be used, and although fresh plants have greater medicinal value, dried herbs are available all year round from health food shops. Dried herbs generally lose their potency after 6-7 months, while roots, bark and seeds can be kept for up to three years.

Infusions: For drinking and external use, infusions are made just like tea, either in a cup, or in a pot kept especially for the purpose. It's important that the infusion be kept covered for 10-15 minutes before drinking. Since many flower infusions can be bitter, honey can be used as a sweetener. Use one teaspoon of dried flowers per cup of boiling water (use two-three times the amount of fresh flowers). Infusions can be drunk as tea, or use cold as a lotion or compress. An infusion is made in the same way as a pot of tea; strained through a muslin sieve and drunk while hot. The standard dosage for herbal infusions is one teacup three times a day.

Chamomile: A soothing calming drink that aids sleep; as a lotion to ease irritated skin.

Elder flower: Soothes colds and fever; or use as a complexion lotion.

Hawthorn: Use fresh flowers as a tonic for circulation and insomnia.

Lavender: A cold compress for headaches.

Marigold: Ideal for a soothing skin lotion.

Rosemary: A compress for soothing tension.

Sage: A drink for combating hot flushes and night sweats.

Decoctions: These are made when roots or the hard woody parts of the plant are used and merely pouring boiling water over it is not sufficient to extract the active ingredient. Allow it to simmer for at least 20 minutes and strain through a nylon sieve while hot. If kept in a cool place, a decoction will last a day or two. The standard dosage is one teacup three times a day. Parsley root for digestive properties comes under this heading.

Tinctures: These contain the active ingredient of a plant in alcohol – the most famous being 'rescue remedy'. Tinctures are often preferred to infusions and decoctions because they are more palatable and, after the initial preparation, are quick and easy to use since they can be taken neat or with a little water. Make a standard tincture with one pint of at least 30% proof alcohol (vodka is ideal), and pour over 4ozs of dried herbs. Keep the mixture in a warm place for two weeks and shake daily. Strain the liquid through muslin into a dark, airtight bottle and take 1 teaspoon three times a day. Thyme tinctures for coughs and bronchitis also come under this heading.

Compresses and poultices: These are applied to the outside of the body and are used to treat wounds, skin conditions and strains. A compress is usually applied cold (for example, a bag of frozen peas for bringing out a bruise or a cold teabag for tired eyes); while a poultice is applied as hot as bearable (for drawing a splinter or a boil).

Warning: Most natural herbals can be toxic if taken in excess.

Cupboard Cures

Everyday kitchen cupboard ingredients can also be used for curing little ailments and back in the day, these were automatically administered whenever the need arose. Over-the-counter remedies still cost a fortune and are often no more effective than those old-fashioned cures our grandmothers handed out. Even the witch's or wise woman's modern kitchens might not have those old, evocative smells of yesteryear, but the contents of the kitchen cupboard and larder (if you're lucky enough to have one) should still contain these precious ingredients.

Bicarbonate of Soda

'Bicarb' or baking soda has dozens of uses for minor medical complaints and personal health issues if you run out of a normal healthcare product. Create a breath freshener by adding one teaspoon in half a glass of water, swish, spit and rinse: odours are neutralized, not just covered up. It also serves as an emergency toothpaste. Use as a facial scrub by making a paste of three parts baking soda to one part water. This is gentle enough for daily use rub in a gentle circular motion to exfoliate the skin and rinse clean. Pat baking soda onto your underarms to neutralise body odour and sprinkle in shoes to freshen. 'Bicarb' is a safe and effective antacid to relieve heartburn, sour stomach and/or acid indigestion. It is also standby for anyone suffering from cystitis or urinary tract infection. Take half a teaspoon in an 8fl oz glass of water a few times a day at the first sign of discomfort. For insect bites and bee stings make a paste out of baking soda and water, and apply as a salve onto affected skin.

To Make a Bath Soak

Add 2¼oz of baking soda to your bath to neutralize acids on the skin and help wash away oil and perspiration, it also makes your skin feel very soft. A few tablespoons into the bathwater also helps relieve heat rash, hives, nappy rash and even haemorrhoids – a paste eases chicken pox itching, too. Soothe tired and aching feet by dissolving three tablespoons of baking soda in a tub of warm water and soak feet. Gently scrub.

Bread

Bread was mixed with hot milk to make a poultice and draw out infection. Stale bread was used to make delicious bread and butter pudding that was excellent for the treatment of anyone who was off their food. A classic, convenient and traditional way of using up yesterday's bread and milk.

Bread and Butter Pudding

1 pint whole milk
4 slices white bread, buttered and cut into triangles
1 handful raisins
2 tablespoons caster sugar
2 drops vanilla essence

Heat the oven to 140C/fan 120C/gas Stir half the sugar and vanilla essence into the milk and gently heat. Trim the crusts from the bread, cut into triangles, then place in a large bowl with the raisins. Pour over the custard mixture so all the pieces of bread are coated and leave to soak. Lightly grease a small ovenproof dish with butter, then spoon in the mixture. Cook for 30-35 minutes until there is just a slight wobble in the centre of the custard. Sprinkle the rest of the sugar to cover the surface, then pop under a hot grill for 1-2 minutes until the sugar starts to melt and caramelise.

Cucumber

A slice of cucumber applied to the eyes for 15-20 minutes soothes tired eyes and reduces dark circles and puffiness. Apply cucumber to the skin to provide relief from sunburn. It supplies skin-friendly minerals: magnesium, potassium, silicon and is used extensively as a beauty therapy.

Garlic

Health-wise garlic has antibiotic, anti-fungal, anti-parasitic and antiviral properties; garlic oil is used for treating stings, bites, dysentery, colds and diarrhoea. For cold prevention take one garlic capsule three times a day, while eating a raw garlic clove every day helps prevent constipation. Garlic can be obtained in capsule or tablet form to avoid bad breath caused by raw garlic.

Ginger

Taken in warm milk for a tummy upset, it was also taken to relieve heartburn and morning sickness (or eat a ginger biscuit). Anxiety is lessened by breathing in the aroma of ginger, and it was taken for headaches – half a teaspoon stirred into a glass of warm water. For menstrual cramps, one teaspoon of fresh ginger root was added to a cup of boiling water and left to steep for 10 minutes.

Honey

Honey has many uses and was regarded as a 'sweet antiseptic'. A teaspoon of honey with a slice of lemon added to a glass of hot water is excellent treatment for winter colds and 'flu. Because it has a natural laxative effect, one teaspoon of honey each morning helps to keep you regular and fit. It was also used to treat cuts and grazes if no antiseptic cream was handy. Going back in time, it was used to disinfect and pack serious wounds sustained on the battlefield.

Ice

Wrap an ice cube in cling film and hold on a pimple for five minutes in every hour after it appears, to reduce redness. Crushed ice in a tea towel (or a bag of frozen peas) is perfect for treating sprains: apply to the affected part until the ice begins to melt and reapply as necessary until the swelling reduces.

Lemon

A glass of lemon juice diluted in hot water is a good way to start the day to help flush the system, as well as treating colds, 'flu and sore throats. For 'age spots' mix one teaspoon of lemon juice with one teaspoon of yoghurt and apply. Leave it on for 30 minutes once a day. It was also considered a good cure for belching if taken in water before eating.

Milk

Hot milk is an old-fashioned comforter and a remedy for insomnia. Milk contains tryptophan, an amino acid use in the production of the brain chemical serotonin, which improves the sense of well-being.

Oats

Eating porridge for breakfast is a good way of lowering cholesterol, but oatmeal was also used in the bath by people suffering from eczema. Water is run over a piece of muslin filled with a few tablespoons of oatmeal, which was said to have a soothing and anti-inflammatory effect.

Cabbage and Oat Face Mask
Two large fresh cabbage leaves
One egg white
Cup of porridge oats

To cure teenage spots overnight (suitable for boys and girls) put the ingredients into a liquidiser and turn to maximum speed until everything turns to a paste. Scrape it out into a clean container with a tight fitting lid and it will keep in the fridge for a couple of days. Use it as a face pack every night. Leave the pack on for about 20 minutes and then rinse off with warm water. Once the skin has cleared use the preparation once a week to keep skin blemish free.

Cabbage leaves can also be used on a wound that refuses to heal or to draw a splinter. Score the leaf lightly and fasten over the bad area with bandage and cling film and leave on overnight.

Onions

Quercetin is the main reason onions are included in so many folk remedies and published herbals, since at least the 16th century, have generally agreed with the diverse traditions about the effectiveness of onions. Red onions include the highest amounts and it can be found mostly on the part closest to the root and in its external rings, which are nearest to the skin; white and yellow onions are recommended in some home remedies. Onions have potent antioxidant, anti-inflammatory, antihistamine and anticholesterol properties and the ability to eliminate the toxins from the body thanks to the strong antibiotic properties. They should be used in their raw form in order to get all of their medicinal benefits; those grown organically and locally are best for homemade remedies.

Onions to Remove an Eye Irritant

Onion will make you cry like nothing else, which makes it great for removing some irritants out of the eye when the tears start to flow. The eye shouldn't come in contact with the onion because it will make things even worse.

Parsley

It was often said that only the wicked could grow parsley and that it was unlucky to give or receive the plant despite it being valued in numerous cures. It is a good cure for bad breath as it contains large amounts of chlorophyll and is one of least calorific herbs with 100g of fresh leaves carrying just 36 calories. Additionally, its leaves carry zero cholesterol and fat, but are rich in anti-oxidants, vitamins, minerals, and dietary fibre. Altogether, the herb helps in controlling blood-cholesterol, and may offer protection from some cancers. Parsley is, perhaps, the richest herbal source for vitamin K, which plays an important role in bone health and in the treatment of Alzheimer's by limiting neuronal damage in the brain.

Potatoes

Potatoes, of any kind, whether they are raw, boiled, peeled, or mashed all have medicinal and healing properties. A widely practised cure for rheumatism involved the simple process of carrying a potato in the pocket. A black eye was often cured by the application of a slice of uncooked potato, as were small burns. Raw potato slices can be placed over burns and insect stings. **Warning: A potato that has developed a greenish tinge should be avoided as this can produce a toxic effect.**

Salt

Gargling twice a day with a cup of warm water and half a teaspoon of salt helps relieve sore mouths and throats. Bathing the affected part in salt dissolved in water warm is an effective treatment for cuts and grazes.

Tea

A 'nice cup of tea' was said to be a cure for anything, but it was specifically believed to be a cure for a headache. Black tea with sugar was drunk to alleviate diarrhoea as the tannins in it were believed to reduce inflammation; chamomile tea at night helps insomnia. A black tea footbath was supposed to be good for sweaty feet.

Vinegar

Apple cider vinegar is recommended to combat all sorts of ailments from arthritis and fatigue to night sweats and yeast infections. As a fungus fighter, mix one part white vinegar to four-parts hot water and soak the feet in it for at least 30 minutes twice a day to treat athlete's foot. It also soothes wasp stings and is an odour eliminator. Because it is a bactericide, it is a natural treatment for minor cuts, abrasions and other skin ailments.

Whiskey

A hot whiskey drink made with a shot of Irish whiskey in warm water, a slice of lemon, a teaspoon of sugar and four cloves is said to cure a broken heart. Ten of them will cure anything!

Witch Hazel

The witch hazel water you can buy at any pharmacy is actually a steam distillation of the bark, leaves, and twigs of the shrub itself. To treat cold sores, dab the affected area with soaked gauze and this will help dry out the sore. It can also be used to treat acne, reduce puffiness around the eyes, cure a sore throat, heal a bruise, cleanse and soothe a wound, stop an itch and refresh the skin.

Burn Charm

Say this traditional charm as you run cold water over a burn: *'Three ladies came out of the East;/The one brought fire, the other brought frost/Out fire; in frost./In the name of the Father and Son and Holy Ghost/Amen*. Or better still keep a bottle of distilled witch hazel in the kitchen for small domestic emergences. The instant application of the liquid reduces burning and prevents scarring.

There are dozens of books available on the subject of simple domestic remedies and every budding parish-pump witch, cunning and wise woman should keep one in the kitchen by the cookery books. Preparing a personal medicine chest according to the common ailments of the family is important, but there is little point making a preparation of elderberry salve for piles if no one suffers from them!

In *Memory, Wisdom & Healing*, Gabrielle Hatfield also points out that in general, too much has been made of the link between magic, witchcraft, superstition and plant medicine: 'Once written down, many of the rules for using such plants became distorted. The image of the herb-gatherer only collecting plants at a certain time of the day, and in dark and shady places, has twisted the truth.'

In reality these myths were a smoke-screen to a) preserve the mystique of *The Secret People* and b) to keep the process of gathering the plants a secret. It has been scientifically proven that the properties of plants vary considerably, depending on the time of the season, the growth cycle of the plant, and sometimes the time of day at which it is cut. The accompanying rituals also had some useful purpose in that certain metals coming into contact with the juice of the plant could nullify its usefulness as a healing agent.

Dr Hatfield explains:

The medically active ingredients of plants are often alkaloids which vary in concentration not only with the season and time of day, but also with the habitat in which the individual plants are growing. Many active plant constituents peak in the morning, and in the spring, and at least in some instances it has been shown that their concentration is higher in plants grown in the shade.

Nevertheless, country people still relied on these remedies

rather than go to the doctor and many of those mentioned were still in common use well into the 20th century. As Gabrielle Hatfield also points out: 'How far have we misinterpreted the role of the 'wise man', 'cunning man' or 'wise woman' of the past? Perhaps many of them were the equivalent of [someone's] aunt: well-versed in plant medicines, and therefore able to help family and friends in time of sickness; just this and no more: there may have been no ritual or magic in their home medicines.'

Old Wives' Tales

An 'old wives tale' is a dismissive expression normally used to indicate that a supposed truth is actually a superstition to be ridiculed. Such 'tales' were considered to be unverified claims with exaggerated and inaccurate details, often focussing on 'women's concerns', discouraging unseemly behaviour in children, or folk cures for ailments ranging from a headache to in-growing toenails.

Old Women's Sayings was a song published on 'Broadside' by a number of 19th century printers, the earliest being John Pitts and James Catnach. A broadside was a large sheet of paper printed on one side only. They were usually posters announcing events or proclamations, or simply advertisements. Broadsides are difficult to date accurately since all the printers copied each other's work as a matter of course, but the earliest versions seem to date from c1835.

Draw near and give attention
And you shall hear in rhyme
The old women's saying
In the olden time.
High and low, rich and poor
By daylight or dark
Are sure for to make

Some curious remark
With some foolish idea
Your brains they will bother
For some believes one thing
And some believes another.

Chorus:
These are odds and ends
And superstitious ways
The signs and tokens
Of my grandmother's days.

The first thing you will see
At the house of rich or poor
To keep the witches out
A horseshoe's o'er the door;
Bellows on the table
Cause a row by day and night
If there's two knives across
You are sure to have a fight;
There's a stranger in the grate
Or if the cat should sneeze
Or lay before the fire
It will rain or freeze.

A cinder with a hole
In the middle, is a purse
But a long one from the fire
Is a coffin – which is worse;
A spider ticking in the wall
Is the death-watch at night
A spark in the candle
Is a letter, sure as life;
If your right eye itches

You'll cry till out of breath
A winding sheet in the candle
Is a sure sign of death.

If your left eye itches
You will laugh outright
But the left or right
Is very good at night;
If your elbow itch
A strange bedfellow found
If the bottom of your foot itch
You'll tread on strange ground;
If your knee itch you'll kneel
In a church, that's a good 'un
And if your belly itch
You'll get a lot of pudden.

If your back should itch
I do declare
Butter will be cheap
When the grass grows there
If the dog howl at night
Or mournfully cry
Or if the cock should crow
There will be someone die;
If you stumble up stairs
Indeed I'm no railer
You'll be married to a snob
Or else to a tailor.

A speck on your finger nail
Is a gift that's funny
If your hand itch in the middle
You will get some money;

Spilling of salt
Is anger outright
You will see a ghost if the doors
Should rattle in the night;
If your sweetheart
Dreams of bacon and eggs
She'll have a little boy
That has got three legs.

The cat washing her face
The wind will blow
If the cat licks her foot
It is sure to snow;
Put your gown or your jacket
On, inside out
You will change your luck
And be put to the route [sic]
If your nose itches
You'll get vexed till you jump
If your great toe itch
You'll get a kick in the rump.

If a girl snaps one finger
She'll have a child it seems
And if she snaps two
She's sure to have twins;
And if she snaps eight
Nine, ten, or eleven
It's a chance if she don't
Have twenty and seven;
If you lay with your head
Underneath the clothes
You'll have an ugly old man
What has got no nose.

If you see a star shoot
You'll get what you wish
If a hair gets in your mouth
You'll get as drunk as a fish;
If your little toe itch
You'll be lost in a wave
If you shiver there's somebody
Going over your grave;
If you go under a ladder
You'll have bad luck and fall
And so say bad luck
Is better than none at all;
So to please outright
I have told you in rhyme
The great superstition
Of the olden time.

Many of these sayings passed into family use although some differed around the country. For example, an itchy palm was said to show money was on the way, but some believe it's the right hand, while others say: *'Left hand receive,'* and rub the palm against wood. The explanation for the latter was that the receiver shook hands with the right hand, as they were receiving the 'gift' with their left. 'It works every time,' admitted one country woman. 'It might only be a penny found in the street, but it has to be unexpected.'

In recent years, research has show that more and more of these old superstitions have more than a grain of truth in them, or have detected the logic behind the casual warnings. Whether they are fact or fiction, most people have grown up with their use within the family.

Wart-Charming

Wart-charming was often seen as an independent skill in the

removal of warts from both humans and animals; and there are men and women who have the ability to charm away warts by various ways and means, who are not witches, wise women or cunning-folk. While people nowadays still get warts, it is very unusual to find anyone with their hands covered in them as was often described in previous generations. As *The Guide to Superstitions in Britain and Ireland* explains, wart cures combine procedures. Some are possibly genuinely therapeutic – such as the use of certain plants – and which belong to the world of alternative medicine; on the other hand there are the magical elements – such as the use of charms and chanting.

Therapeutic

Many cures usually call for the wart to be rubbed or anointed with certain organic substance, but once the recommended practise instructs that the substance be disposed of in a certain way it steps over into the magical realm of 'sympathetic magic' and transference.

Magical

The practise of burying the substance used to rub or anoint the wart is probably the most common; the explanation being that as the substance rots, so the warts will waste away. In many cases, however, the treatment relies solely on the charm recited, or the personal power of the charmer. In other cases the charmer merely looked at the warts and did not touch them at all. When the warts duly disappeared, this was taken as proof of the charmer's power.

A charmer can also cure the warts by transferring them on to other people, animals or an inanimate object, but as author Steve Roud comments, from the folklorist's point of view, the buying and selling of warts is one of the most interesting of wart cures. He says: 'Whereas many other cures combine varying degrees of physical and magical elements, the idea that warts can be cured simply by being bought falls squarely into the magical camp.'

There is also the belief among the charmers themselves that to charge money for any treatment will result in the lessening of their power, although some will accept a gift as a token of thanks. Some, particularly those who only treat animals, find that their skills do not apply to humans, or that warts are the only complaint they can treat. To this day, nobody can explain the wart-charming phenomenon except to say that in a large number of cases it works.

Chapter Four

The Fortune-Teller

If there was one mysterious element of *The Secret People* that intrigued their neighbours, it was the skill of foretelling the future. The local fortune-teller would probably have been pestered by young girls in the village about romance; or their mothers quietly wanting to know if there was the likelihood of any money in the offing; a father might consult her about stolen property or to remove ill-wishing caused by a neighbour. To glean the answers she (or he) would probably use a favoured method of divination, or privately resort to magic.

The scope of fortune-telling is similar to the practice of divination, except the difference is that divination is the term used for predictions considered part of a ritual invoking outside influences, while fortune-telling implies a less serious or informal setting. The most common methods used for fortune-telling by *The Secret People* included tasseography (reading tea leaves in a cup); cartomancy (fortune-telling with playing cards) or possibly tarot reading; crystallomancy (reading of a crystal ball); chiromancy (palmistry, reading of the palms); lampadomancy or candle magic...and pendulum reading.

Probably much of the 'telling' was pure informed guesswork based on a thorough knowledge of the neighbours' secrets, since little escapes notice in a village environment – even today!

Folklore and Superstition

'It is the hardest thing in the world to shake off superstitious prejudices: they are sucked in as it were with our mother's milk; and growing up with us at a time when they take the fastest hold and make the most lasting impressions, become so interwoven into our very constitution, that the strongest good sense is required to disengage ourselves from them,' naturalist and ornithologist Gilbert White observed back in 1788.

There were numerous superstitions and old wives' tales that were believed to herald some future event and these have come down to us in the form of love charms, when in fact most can be adapted to elicit other information. Simple methods such as **botanomancy** – divination that may include the burning of plants or leaves and foretelling events through the ashes, or smoke generated from the burning or smouldering leaves; even blowing seeds from a dandelion 'clock'. None of these simple methods required a fortune-teller to interpret the outcome and are part of our native folklore. For example:

Capnomancy: Divination by the patterns in the smoke made by throwing various botanical material into the flames or onto hot coals. If the smoke rises straight up the answer is favourable, but if it hovers near the ground it's a negative sign.

Causimonancy: Divination by throwing flammable objects into a fire or onto hot coals. The answer is given in the way and object burns. If it burns quickly the answer is yes; if it smoulders and burns slowly the answer is unfavourable.

Daphnomancy: Using smoke of burning branches of laurel to answer questions and forecast upcoming events. If the branches crackled the answer was favourable; if the fire was quiet or the smoke did not rise but hung close to the ground, it was considered a negative omen. Bear in mind that the smoke from burning laurel can have a hallucinatory effect.

Sideromancy: Divination by the interpreting of the twisting and smouldering of pieces of straw placed on a red-hot surface. The twirling, 'dancing' motions of the sticks of straw were used to foretell the future or interpret omens.

Similarly, there are dozens of superstitions and magical charms associated with eggs. For example, divination with eggs – dropping egg white into a bowl of water and observing/interpreting the shapes – is known as **oomancia**. The egg shell should be pierced with a needle to allow the white to drip out, but do not crack the egg open, and beware if any yolk emerges or the reading will be invalid. To ensure the fertility of seed grain, it was the custom to place an iron nail (for protection) and an egg at the bottom of any container of this precious commodity.

Eggs also make a protective gift for a new mother and baby; give an even number of eggs for a boy, and an odd number for a girl. When the first egg is broken, the mother should smear the face of the child with some of the white; alternatively a protective symbol can be drawn on the forehead. Although the giving and receiving of eggs is generally associated with Easter, this is an ancient pagan custom and can be celebrated as such.

Practically all native plants, flowers, trees, birds and animals have one superstition or folk-tale attached, so *The Secret People* had plenty of elements from which to draw their predictions.

Divination

Divination is one of the oldest forms of fortune-telling – the attempt to discover the future, or any hidden knowledge by means of interpreting signs. As Kathryn Paulsen in *The Complete Book of Magic and Witchcraft* points out, however, there is a fine line between passively reading the future, whether by observing chance omens, or setting out to divine it by studying particular objects (fortune-telling), and attempting to change the future magically (witchcraft).

Cartomancy or Fortune-Telling with Playing Cards and Tarot Cards

Forms of cartomancy appeared soon after playing cards were first introduced into Europe in the 14th century and it was the most popular form of providing fortune-telling card readings throughout the 18th, 19th and 20th centuries. Certain cards have traditionally been regarded as unlucky. The ace of spades is the most ominous, but several other cards also had bad reputations, such as the four of clubs that was said to represent the Devil's four-post bedstead.

There are a number of popular card layouts – some using all 52 cards in the pack, others using only a few. Generally speaking, the seeker shuffles the deck before the cards are placed on the table and the seeker selects a single card they wish to represent themself. Regardless of the deck or layout, the influence of the different suits remain the same:

- Hearts are the lucky cards and indicate good fortune and success in business, career and love.
- Clubs are the cards of success, with a strong connection to money, prosperity and ambition. Depending on the placement they may also foretell business problems.
- Diamonds are indicative of influences outside of the personal and other claims on the seeker's time and energy.
- Spades are regarded as a caution and may warn of unforeseen difficulties in the seeker's life.

Although the tarot is an ancient form of fortune-telling, it was not in common circulation in Britain until the 20th century with its 78 card deck being separated into the Major and the Minor Arcana. The 'Tarot de Marseille' is one of the standards from which many tarot decks of the 19th century and later are derived although the name was coined c1889 by the French occultist Papus and popularised in the 1930s by the French cartomancer Paul

Marteau, who used this collective name to refer to a variety of closely related designs that were being made in the city of Marseille.

The images on the popular Rider-Waite deck were drawn by artist Pamela Colman Smith following the instructions of mystic and occultist Arthur Edward Waite and were originally published by the Rider Company in 1910. The deck departs from the earlier tarot design with its use of scenic pip cards and the adjustment of the Strength and Justice cards. These two decks were the earliest tarot cards generally available outside the occult community at the time and *The Secret People* would probably have still used a standard 52-card deck for their readings.

Crystalomancy or Reading of a Crystal Sphere
A method using the traditional 'crystal ball' of the gypsy fortune-teller, but many local fortune-tellers would not have been able to afford such an expensive commodity. There is evidence of the use of crystal balls as a means of divination in medieval times, and this form of scrying produces the most satisfactory results. Dr John Dee, psychic to Elizabeth I, used a crystal ball and a blackened mirror (now in the British Museum) for the same purpose.

The reading is usually carried out in a darkened room with a light bouncing off the crystal ball. The gazer stares into the crystal ball until a vision appears, which is then interpreted to provide an answer to the seeker's question. The points of light reflected from the ball's polished surface serve to hold the attention of the gazer and then to fix the eye, until gradually the optic nerve becomes so fatigued that it finally ceases to transmit to the sensorium the impression made from without, and begins to respond to the reflex action proceeding from the brain of the gazer.

Magic Crystals, Sacred Stones describes a method of placing the crystal on a table and protecting it from the reflections of surrounding objects by means of a velvet screen. Seven candle-sticks should be placed in front of the screen. The candles are then lit, the room being otherwise in complete darkness. The gazer should seat themselves with the hands laying flat upon the table either side of the crystal. Gaze fixedly into the crystal for half an hour or longer and the light from the candles will certainly ensure a multitude of light points in the crystal. Sometimes the image is distinctly perceptible on or about the surface of the crystal, while at other times the visual perception will be rather indefinite and clouded, although accompanied by strong mental impressions.

Chiromancy or Palmistry, Reading of the Hands

Crossing a gypsy's palm with silver was a familiar event at the village fete since reading someone's palm is pretty cut-and-dried despite the fact it is considered one of the most ancient forms of divination. Palmistry continued to be popular throughout the Middle Ages especially with the cunning-folk as they moved around the country.

There are complex variations to reading the fingers, hands and palms, but generally speaking, the palmist will take the left (or less prominent) hand to indicate potential, and right reveals what has happened in forming that person's character. The three lines found on almost all hands, and generally given most weight by palmists are: the Heart Line representing love is found towards the top of the palm under the fingers; the Head Line, starting at the edge of the palm under the index finger and flowing across the palm towards the outside edge; and the Life Line that extends from the edge of the palm above the thumb and travels in an arc towards the wrist. In addition to this are the many other lines and mounts to take into consideration and which form an important part of the reading.

Lampadomancy and Candle Magic

There are lots of superstitions surrounding candles and many of them concerned with death.

A blue flame warns that ghosts or spirits were near. Shakespeare alludes to this in *Richard III* when the King observes: 'The lights burn blue. It is now dead midnight.' Although a bright spark on the candle wick indicates a letter about to arrive. In *Pagan Portals: Candle Magic*, Lucya Starza shares this simple method for using a candle to bring about your desire:

> Now think of something you want to wish for. Keep it simple and try to sum it up in one word; *health, wealth, happiness, love, success, security, justice* are all good words to use. Take the tealight out of its casing and scratch that word onto the side or bottom. If you want a new job or a new home, just scratch 'job' or 'home'. Short and simple is best. While you are inscribing your word, concentrate on a mental picture of what your life will be like when your wish comes true. (This technique is called 'visualisation' and it draws on the powers of the imagination to help you see clearly what you want and work towards getting it...) Hold the candle in your hands for a moment or two after you have finished carving your wish, but continue the visualisation... Light the candle. Ideally, let it burn down all in one go, but that isn't always practical and it isn't safe to leave a lit candle unattended. An alternative is to burn the candle over several evenings until it is finished. One final bit of advice – don't keep wondering whether your spell will work. When you aren't actually doing the spell, try to keep it out of your thoughts. Carry on with your normal life and let the magic happen. If you keep worrying about whether your wish will come true there's a chance you will disperse the magic through fretting about it.

Lampadomancy uses the flames from an oil lamp or candle to

foresee the future. The term owes to Greek origins, *lampas* which means light and *manteia* which means prophecy. Sometimes a ritual specifically calls for three identical lighted candles placed in the shape of a triangle – often a fourth would be added. The shapes and flickering movements of the flames are then observed by the seer who predicts the future.

Radiesthesia or Pendulum Predictions

Regardless of the object suspended, it typically has a special significance for the reader and the method is a variation of dowsing often used to locate people, information and articles. Because of how it operates, the pendulum can only answer questions that are phrased so that the answer is either 'yes' or 'no', so it cannot be asked to accurately predict the future. The pendulum is still used to locate missing property, people and pets and is uncannily successful; not to mention its use in finding water and minerals.

Radiesthesia is also commonly known as dowsing. It is regarded principally as a mystic art that has many facets and applications. Basically, it is the process of locating the presence of an object, or assessing the energy given off by a subject, with an implement known as a dowsing rod, which is a Y-shaped hazel, beech, or alder branch or a copper rod. Dowsers may also use a pendulum, which is often weighted with a crystal or some other heavy weight. The British Society of Dowsers was formed in the 1930s and the art was re-named radiesthesia by French priest Alex Bouly, derived from the Latin words radiation and perception. However, to many people it is still called dowsing. Modern practitioners of radiesthesia claim that their art uses a 'sense' that was once commonly acknowledged, but that has been lost with time.

Whatever it's called, a pendulum is a very powerful and reliable tool for accessing higher guidance and for getting accurate answers to any question. The answers are given in the form of a pre-determined reaction – the pendulum swinging deosil for 'yes' and widdershins for 'no' or swinging backwards and forwards for a positive response and in a circle to denote a negative one. Although it only takes a few minutes to learn how to use a pendulum, it can take a bit of practise to master the art of pendulum dowsing for maximum reliability.

Tasseography (Reading Tea Leaves in a Cup)
Reading the tea leaves and coffee grounds was taken quite seriously in the past and widely popular for about 200 years. An advertisement in the *Dublin Weekly Journal* dated 1726 was for the 'famous Mrs Cherry' who professed to be an expert at the 'occult science of tossing coffee grounds'. Most of the early references refer to coffee grounds, but gradually tea-leaf reading became the most popular. Instructions for reading the leaves were published regularly throughout the 19th and 20th centuries in small pamphlets devoted to the subject.

Ideally, choose a wide teacup that is white on the inside. Use a fine loose-leaf tea (some readers give the seeker the choice of blends) and do not use a strainer when pouring the tea into the cup. The person who is asking the question needs to drink the tea and it is from that teacup the reading will be taken. Ask the person to drink until there is about a teaspoon of liquid left in the cup and ask them to think of the three most prominent questions. Have the person swish the cup to the left three times, holding it in their left hand, then to gently turn the cup upside down on the saucer to allow the liquid to drain out. Still with the left hand, have them turn the cup three times to the left while upside down on the saucer, holding their hands on the cup in that position, and to think about the important questions again for a count of seven. The cup should be handed to the reader to divine the answers from the leaves left clinging to the inside of the cup.

Whatever results are given by any form of divination, it is important to realise that the future is not fixed and a reading

indicating problems to be faced offers a warning of what will come to pass if appropriate steps are not taken to avert the trouble.

Casting of Lots

Sortilege systems have been around ever since the first pebbles or animal bones were cast by a tribal medicine man to determine the future. All forms of 'lot casting' takes place when an object is thrown into the air, dropped onto a surface, or selected from a bag or box in a process of random selection. Crystallomancy, for example, is an ancient practice of casting lots using small stones or crystals and unlike crystalomancy, by which images or messages are received by meditating in a crystal ball, the results depend on the placement of the stones. This method requires specific crystals (or stones) being cast onto a circle marked out with divisions for the past present and future. The 'lots' are deciphered according to the influence of the stone and its placement within the circles. The following method is taken from my book *Magic Crystals, Sacred Stones*:

Try this Exercise:
When sitting on a garden seat or park bench look at the stones around your feet. At first glance this will probably appear as ordinary gravel, or aggregate from a builders' merchant or garden centre — smooth pebbles or rough-quarried stone. Having said that, pebbles and stones are to be found everywhere: in the shallow streambed, on the sandy banks of an inland river, turned over in a ploughed field, on the beach, or even dug up our own gardens.

Each stone may be discovered under unusual circumstances, or it may be something that we just feel the need to pick up and possess. Whatever the reason for our selection, these stones will begin to form the basis for our magical collection and because these small stones are 'special', you will remember exactly where and under what circumstances you found them. Keep them together in a tall glass jar or goldfish bowl until you have sufficient quantity to utilise for magical use and keep a note of each one in a magical journal or diary if you have a poor memory.

The next step is to create a linen cloth for divinational purposes – using three circles to represent the past, present and future. Take a large white linen napkin and in the centre draw a circle the size of a large dinner plate; now place a tea plate in the centre of the first circle and draw a second circle; finally take a teacup or mug and draw a third circle inside the second circle. The centre circle represents Past, the inner circle the Present and the outer circle the Future. Now select twelve small pebbles from your collection and remember that each stone has been discovered under unusual circumstances, or is one that you just felt the need to pick up and possess and will, therefore, influence your 'reading'.

Holding the twelve stones cupped between the palms of your hands, drop them onto the cloth and observe how they scatter. Disregard any that fall outside the outer circle. Those in the centre circle will refer to the past, which may have a bearing on the present and the future. The stones in the middle circle refer to the here and now; those in the outer circle are linked to the future. Now begin your first reading by identifying what each stone means to you, i.e. good or bad news. Remember, the 'lots' are deciphered according to the influence of the stones and their placement within the circles – revealing the future as relating to the past and the present.

The most remarkable thing about divination is its overwhelming success – but before setting yourself up as a 'seer' for other people, you will need to create a separate set of stones from those used for your own personal readings to avoid unwanted psychic transference.

Charms and Spell-Casting

The most popular spells or charms performed by *The Secret People* would have been love spells, charms for attracting money and protection from malignant spirits or neighbours. Local wise women would probably been driven barmy by silly village girls demanding to know who they were going to marry, which probably accounts for the large number of 'love-spells' included in our native folklore and addressed to various different saints. These were simple actions that required no formal ritual and future marriage prospects could be determined by:

> Naming two acorns, one for yourself and one for your sweet-heart, and dropping them into a basin of water. Marriage was a certainty if they floated close together.

The most popular time for love spells was St Agnes Eve on the 20th January. From 1696 comes this version from Aubrey's *Miscellanies*:

> The women have several magical secrets, handed down to them by tradition, for this purpose...take a row of pins and pull out every one, one after another, saying a Pater Noster (Our Father), or sticking a pin in your sleeve, and you will dream of him, or her, you shall marry ...

> *And on sweet St Agnes night*
> *Please you with the promis'd sight*
> *Some of husbands, some of lovers*
> *Which an empty dream discovers.*

Or peel an apple, taking care that the peel remains in one long piece, then throw the peel over your shoulder. The shape it takes will resemble the initial of the future lover's name. Ideally this should be done on 28th October on the feast day of Saints Simon and Jude and accompany the action with the following rhyme...although why the patron saint of lost causes was evoked for romance it is impossible to say:

St Simon and Jude, on you I intrude
By this paring I hold to discover
Without any delays, to tell me this day
The first letter of my own true lover.

Or sticking pins in an apple, a golden pippin for preference – nine new pins in the eye and nine in the stem – tying it in a left garter and placing it under the pillow, and then get into bed backwards reciting:

Good St Thomas do me right
And bring my love to me this night
That I might view him face to face
And in my arms may him embrace

Another method was to hang your smock before the fireplace and await for the arrival of an apparition of the man you're due to marry to come in and turn it for you.

On St Mark's eve, at twelve o'clock,
The fair maid will watch her smock,
To find her husband in the dark,
By praying unto good St Mark.

To Protect your House

A widespread superstition required that on St Martin's Day (11th November of the Old Calendar) blood be spilt. In many parts of the country, on the eve of the feast of St Martin, a cock or hen was killed, and a little of its blood sprinkled on the door jambs, the threshold and the hearth. The bird was eaten the next day. The sprinkling was reputed to bring good luck for the coming year. In earlier times November was the month when cattle that would not be kept over winter would be slaughtered – hence the Anglo-Saxon name of *Blod-monath*, or blood-month. A modern substitute could be the liquid obtained when defrosting a chicken intended for dinner the next day.

A simpler charm required that at each corner of the house should be buried one each of four pebbles or precious stones, and four silver coins. In this case, 'precious' stones could refer to pieces of agate, quartz or jasper; the ideal silver coins would be old six penny pieces that were minted between 1551 and 1970.

To Locate Missing Belongings

Even non-Christians offer up a quick prayer to St Anthony to help them find missing possessions. Remember that the old grimoires frequently evoked the saints' help in their spells. For example:

> *Saint Anthony, who received from God the special power of restoring lost things, grant that I may find (mention your petition) which has been lost. As least restore to me peace and tranquillity of mind, the loss of which has afflicted me even more than my material loss.*

Using a Bible and Key

Widely practised and implicitly trusted, the Bible and front-door key were used to locate lost or stolen property.

In order to find out the thief, tie the key to the Bible, placing it very carefully on the 18th verse of the 50th psalm. Two persons must then hold up the book by the bow of the key, and first repeat the name of the suspected thief, and then the verse from the psalm. If the Bible moves, the suspected person is considered guilty; if it does not move, innocent.

Money-Drawing Spell

The first thing to understand when mixing money and magic is that the more you wish for, the less likely it will come true. Spells for wealth will only bring what a witch *needs*, or it will offer an opportunity to improve your circumstances – but never a winning lottery ticket!

Create a small talisman using a symbol for money – £ or $ or € – together with three coins of the appropriate currency in different denominations. Draw a circle on a piece of clean paper and write inside the reason for the 'need' – for example: rent, vet's bill, school uniform, etc together with the appropriate currency symbol. Place the paper in a small packet together with the coins and seal them into a small package; focus on the bill to be paid and pass the package three time through the flame of a yellow candle, visualising money dropping into your open hand and then say: 'Thank you!'

A talisman should only be kept for as long as the spell is supposed to work, so once the money has been received, dismantle the talisman with a vote of thanks and burn the components. The coins should be given to a charity as an added incentive for more to come your way.

Remember the old saying about being careful about what you ask for – you might just get it! Also beware of asking for more than is needed and keep an open mind about how any money difficulties might be resolved – a leaflet dropped through the door offering to buy broken bits of gold jewellery netted an immediate payment of £200 and came just at the right time!

Chapter Five

The Countryman

As E W Martin wrote in the original *The Secret People*:

> In the village there is always the illusion that one can reach out and touch the past – it is there as a presence in the weathered walls of grey churches, in living festivals and a way of life ... Time does not appear to work its will so rapidly or finally. In any scrutiny of the village the weight of centuries of history is always an imponderable factor...

A true countryman is the last link with our hunter-gatherer ancestors: he takes a rabbit or pigeon for the pot and forages for wild food in season. He understands the language and movements of both wild and domesticated creatures, and can foretell the weather; he may not be a landowner, but his love of the land is bred in the bone.

In using these old country remedies, recipes and charms, we are reaching out and touching a peasant past that can be traced back to the Middle Ages and beyond. These are, of course, oral traditions and over time, much gets distorted in the telling, especially if being passed on to an 'outsider'. Although specific details were rarely written down, this knowledge must be accurate to avoid accidents. For example, the plant comfrey has been used since ancient times as a poultice to treat sprains and help heal broken bones, hence it's old-fashioned name of 'knit-bone'. A Romany, who was being consulted by Dr Gabriel Hatfield about wild herbs, was horrified that the leaves were being given as a herbal tea since it was common knowledge that the leaves were toxic. Used in the traditional way the remedy was perfectly safe, but the modern 'secondary' use of the plant was inaccurate. 'Oral traditions can be remarkably accurate, sometimes more so than the written word, which is subject to copyist's errors, misinterpretation and misrepresentation,' observes Dr Hatfield as a result of her own research. 'Once committed to print, information takes on an authority which it does not always deserve. Any error once appearing in print has a tendency to be repeated almost indefinitely.'

For the countryman, however, all these little snippets of useful intelligence were common knowledge and oral tradition can be surprisingly resilient in remote rural places. And often a few moments quiet contemplation, resting with arms folded on top of a farm gate watching lambs in springtime, a fox hunting for insects, or a herd of grazing cows is all a person needs to 'feel well within himself'.

Seedtime

For our agricultural forebears, particularly those of Celtic blood, there were only two seasons in the year: summer and winter, seedtime and harvest. Summer began at Beltaine when wheat was sown and the cattle turned out to graze; and ended at Samhain, which was the end of the harvest and start of winter when the cattle returned to the fold...and nowhere is this rural calendar more evident than in the 12th century church of St Mary in Ripple in the West Country.

The annual round of country life in the Middle Ages is the subject of a remarkable series of 14th century misericords – the carved backs of choir seats – in St Mary's church. The carvings, believed to be by local craftsmen, add up to a country calendar with religious overtones, showing the tasks of husbandry month by month. Altogether the carvings represent a fascinating glimpse of country living 600 years ago and despite it being hardier then, the essentials of the farmer's year were much the same as they are now. And, as is so often found in old rural churches, the vast majority of English misericords dating from the 14th and 15th centuries are most often depictions of secular or pagan images and scenes, entirely at odds with the Christian iconography and aesthetic that surround them.

The winter occupation of the countryman was the back-breaking task of ditching, because as time goes by the ditches that run along the boundary of the hedge bank fills with decaying plants and dead wood. The traditional way was for the ditcher to come along with a long-handled shovel and scoop out everything, throwing it all onto the bank. The hedger's trade was often linked to the ditcher's, slashing out briars and brambles, cutting back thorn and weaving a permanent barrier to a neighbour's livestock and providing shelter for a wintering animals and arable fields.

The Ripple Misericords

January: Collecting dead boughs for fire wood
February: Hedging and ditching
March: Sowing
April: Bird scaring
May: Crops blessed
June: Hawking scene

At this time of the year, neighbours turned out to help with the haymaking and kept an anxious eye on the weather because a sudden downpour would mean the whole field would have to be re-raked and turned. This process could go on for several days until the hay could be carted off to the farmyard for storing.

It could be made all the worse by biting insects and the awful irritation when small seeds worked their way down into a man's heavy woollen vest. When the first raindrops began to spatter down, long-bodied rainflies emerged from the ditch to drink blood and inflict severe pain ...
[*English Country Traditions*, Ian Niall]

Harvest

From seed time to harvest *The Secret People* must work to Nature's plan and August and September were the months of fulfilment. Spring-birth, winter-death and in between the harvest: and so important was this part of the farming calendar that once upon a time men were given battlefield leave to return home to get in the harvest.

'Gleaning' was also an important element of the harvest: the collecting of leftover crops from fields after they had been commercially harvested or from fields where it was not profitable to harvest. In 18th century England, gleaning was a legal right for cottagers and in a small village community the sexton would often ring a church bell at eight o'clock in the morning and again at seven in the evening to tell the gleaners when to begin and end work. This 'common law' effectively ceased after a legal case in 1788 held that gleaning was a 'privilege' only, and not a right, and that the poor of a parish had no legal right to glean and that to do so such was trespass. Nevertheless, the conditions of farm workers even up to the 1890s made gleaning an essential part of their livelihood.

The Ripple Misericords
July: Lammas (loaf mass) when the first corn was cut
August: Reaping
September: Corn for malting
October: Corns for pigs
November: Pig killing
December: Spinning by the fire

The Secret People had a strong bond with the land, even if it wasn't their own and they knew the heartbeat of the seasons. They understood the movement of birds and animals, and the growing cycle of plants and trees by instinct; they took what they needed to survive and left the rest. Country-lore was something that was instilled into everyone who moved around the fields and woods from childhood, as a form of protection against the dangers that lurked in the hedgerows and stream beds. And most of us survived!

Unfortunately, that countryside described for forty years by the pen of the legendary Ian Niall in a weekly 'Countryman's Notes' for *Country Life* magazine no longer exists; and those who write about it are, more often than not, folk who can never really lay claim to being 'of the country'.

Livestock and Wildlife

Folk-medicine didn't just apply to humans as numerous books on country ways will attest. Gabrielle Hatfield in *Memory, Wisdom and Healing: The History of Domestic Plant Medicine* observed: 'Did our forebears possess a greater instinctive knowledge of food and medicines, akin to that still seen in animals? Horses and cattle will seek out particular plants when they are ill: domestic dogs eat grass to make themselves sick when they have stomach problems.' In her research into domestic plant remedies (for which she won the Michaelis-Jena Ratcliffe Prize for Folklore), Dr Hatfield records instances of sheep seeking out particular plants if they were off-colour, and horses stripping the bark from trees or eating mown nettles as a tonic. Animals played an important part in *The Secret People's* lives...

Cattle: Cattle were highly regarded by the Celts, being the most important animal for their sustenance and welfare and also a basis for wealth and prestige. The highlight of the modern countryman's year was the local cattle show and, as competitive as it was, he took less satisfaction in triumphing over a stranger at a neighbouring show if he had won a smaller prize at his local event. He took a pride in his stock and even today, when the local show is on, he and his family, as well as his men, take the day off, dress themselves up and enjoy the occasion. Most rural superstitions concerning cattle relate to the weather lore and there is a great deal about changeling cattle and magical cows in British folklore, but for *The Secret People* there is no more gratifying sight than a herd of cows peacefully grazing a summer meadow.

Sheep: Sheep play little part in rural superstitions apart from being creatures of annual sacrifice, but to meet a flock of sheep at the beginning of a journey is a sign that the trip will be successful. Peaceful sheep lying in a field are believed to herald fine weather, but rain is on the way if they are restless and bleat without apparent reason. If sheep gnash their teeth during the autumn round-up, the winter will be hard; if at any other time, bad weather is on the way. Sheep were often involved in folk-cures: children with whooping-cough were thought to be cured by letting a sheep breathe on them. Sufferers from consumption were once advised to walk around a sheepfold many times a day, beginning early in the morning.

Pigs: By contrast, pigs featured in a large number of country superstitions including being prone to witchcraft and ill-wishing – as all farm animals were. Pigs were often considered unlucky if encountered as someone was setting out on a journey. It is still commonly believed that pigs cannot swim, because their trotters cut their throats if they try. When pigs are restless or carrying straw in their mouths, a storm is on the way. One superstition to get rid of warts involved rubbing a peeled apple on the afflicted area and feeding it to a pig.

Cats: According to superstition cats were viewed with far more suspicion than affection in the good old days, hence the belief in them being witches' familiars. Although often contradictory, there are more superstitions about cats than any other domestic animal, and although dogs are also believed to have their 'uncanny' side (seeing ghosts, sensing danger and death), this is nothing compared to the range of beliefs about cats, according to *The Penguin Guide to Superstitions in Britain and Ireland*. 'In the great witchcraft trials of the 17th century and in stories about the more humble local village witches of later periods, the chosen companion could be any small animal, and cats only became the dominant species in the late 19th century.'

Birds: These feature widely in British superstition and any unusual behaviour exhibited by them was said to be ominous especially if it appeared to single out a particular person. For *The Secret People* this would be taken as a warning to avert impending trouble: 'When a man is in trouble a bird will always haunt him. He will see that bird wherever he goes.' If the warning was ignored then the 'trouble' would follow. Needless to say, particular species had their own traditions – some birds such as robins, wrens, swallows and martins were protected from harm, while others such as the yellowhammer were killed on sight. Some were often dreaded – owls hooting after dark, single magpies – others like the cuckoo were welcomed if the circumstances were right. A wild bird coming into the house was often seen as a death omen.

Hens: If found roosting in the morning hens are said to be foretelling a death, usually that of the farmer or someone in his household and a hen entering the house was an omen that a visitor would arrive. A hen that cackles near a house is supposed to be forecasting a death, and any hen that persistently cackles is said to have 'got the Devil in her' and should be killed before she takes to destroying her eggs and teaches the other hens to do the same. It is said to be unlucky for a hen to lay an even number of eggs and you would be well advised to remove one from a sitting bird. When a cockerel crowed to welcome the dawn all ghosts and evil spirits had to return to the underworld. A cock crowing in the evening was an omen of bad weather; and if it called during the night hours there would be a death in the family. Crowing at other times was often a warning against misfortune. If a cock crowed while perched on a gate, or at nightfall, the next day would be rainy.

Rooks: Despite the annual culling, rooks seem to like living close to humans, although the onslaught of Dutch elm disease killed off their natural building sites. Being gregarious by nature, they build close to one another, renovating old nests in early spring and quarrelling over sticks as well as the nests themselves. It was said that rooks could detect the disease in a tree and would move on to another clump in which to nest. They moved, but their habits have never changed and they still have their battles and squabbles; they fight and tumble earthwards for fun and fly back to high branches to complain and shout. Being part of the crow family, rooks were often seen as messengers.

Owls: According to *The Penguin Guide to Superstitions of Britain and Ireland*, owls were generally disliked and feared, and their screech was a proverbial death omen – especially if there was a sick person in the house. This interpretation of the owl has a very long history, from Chaucer's Parliament of Fowls (c1380) *'The oule eke, that of deth the bode bringeth'* to numerous writers of 16th and 17th centuries for whom the owl, raven and howling dog were the stock motifs signalling horror and tragedy – instantly recognised by audiences and readers. Owls were also in identified with witches. In literary productions they often provided one of the ingredients in the witches' cauldron, but in traditional witchcraft they were also seen as messengers.

Toads and Frogs: These were widely regarded as having magical and curative powers, which led to them being used in various ways to cast or counter spells. A number of traditions relate to there being a particular bone in a toad's body which, if located and removed in the right way, would confer important power on its owner. This bone is regularly cited as being the key to the 'Horseman's Word' that involved an uncanny mastery over horses. The belief in the power of this bone has been around in Britain for a long time and Reginald Scott mentions it in his *Discoverie of Witchcraft* (1584).

Bees: As countryman, Ian Niall observed that even the humblest cottager knows when he goes to 'take the honey' that the taste depends on the season. If there was an early spring and a great abundance of blossom the beekeeper may taste honey that came from the apple tree overlaid with a hint of sycamore and field maple. If he lives near the moorland the honey will be dark and heavy from the heather. 'Honey has the same quality as wine. It can never be exactly the same again because that precise sequence of summer days will never be repeated.' The most common belief surrounding bees is that they are very sensitive and censorious creatures. They are quick to take offence if not treated with respect and know what is going on in the human world in which they take a keen interest; neither will they be bought or sold, and can only be obtained by barter. A bee (other than a normal hive bee) flying into the house meant good news was on the way, or in some parts of the country that a stranger would shortly arrive...an earlier superstition dating to around c1050 saw bees entering the house as a death omen. The most common belief was that they should be informed of any major change of circumstances in the owner's family, and in particular of any death or they would leave. The widespread custom of 'telling the bees' about major family events is still carried out among modern-day beekeepers.

Horses and Hounds

The horsemen were the big men on the farm. They kept in

with each other and had secrets. They were a whispering lot. And if you disturbed them in a room where the horse medicine was, it was covered up double quick. They made the horses obey with a sniff from a rag which they kept in their pockets. Caraway seeds had something to do with it, I believe, although others say different.

So recorded Ronald Blythe in *Akenfield*, his famous account of village life in the 1960s.

He was, of course, referring to the 'horse whisperers'; that mysterious brotherhood of men who bear no resemblance to those animal behaviourists of today's popular television. The true 'whisperer' kept his secrets hidden. There is an account in my book *Shaman Pathways: Black Horse, White Horse* that recalls a former racehorse trainer and countryman's experience of one of these remarkable and elusive men.

I first heard about George A from my farrier and from certain other trainers in Newmarket because at the time, I owned and ran the public equine swimming pool in Newmarket and was responsible for the fitness development swimming programmes to combat un-soundness and training problems in racehorses... No one was ever allowed to go into the stable or box while George 'looked' at a horse. Needless to say, everyone tried to find a chink in the wall, or stood with an ear pressed against the door in an attempt to find out exactly what went on inside. Sometimes it took five minutes, at other times half an hour, but the only thing we ever heard was silence... There are dozens of stories about George's ability from the length and breadth of the country but no one had any doubts that it was anything other than a genuine gift. As a result, he was treated with a great deal of respect by the racing fraternity...

It was once thought that whooping cough could be cured by going to the stables and inhaling the breath of a horse; being breathed upon by a piebald horse, or riding upon its back, was another supposed cure. Horse-hairs, chopped very finely and fed to a child in bread and butter, were thought to be a certain cure for worms, and the horse-spurs (calluses which appear on the sides of a horse's leg) were believed in the 18th century to be a cure for cancer if dried, ground and drunk frequently with new milk.

Horseshoes and Horse Brasses

Horse brasses were originally designed to protect horses from evil spirits and older ones often incorporate ancient mystical symbols. The practice originated about 5,000 years ago and examples of these talismans have been found across Europe and Asia. The metal was kept highly polished and shiny so that light would dazzle any malignant spirits and drive them off. The most common symbols were acorns, birds, beasts, flowers, hearts and the swastika – all of which have their own magical associations.

Ronald Blythe wrote: 'The blacksmith's shop in most villages is now either a garage, a smart cottage called The Olde Forge or a forlorn lean-to still redolent of horse musk and iron, its roof gradually slithering down to the couch grass mat which covers the yard...' and yet there is still magic in the air. Horseshoes have long been considered harbingers of luck, and any cast shoe should be taken home and nailed over the main entrance to the house or barn. In some parts of the country, a cast horseshoe should be spat on before you make a wish, and then thrown over the left shoulder. Do not look back or the wish will not come true.

A horseshoe was sometimes given as a symbolic payment for a piece of land and it was the special symbol of Bride, the Celtic goddess of blacksmithing. Iron has always been thought to be a very special metal with the power to break enchantments and disperse negative energies – so the horseshoe served a dual purpose. Should anyone be lucky enough to find an old iron horseshoe it should be treasured as it has been created in the sacred fire of the forge and made from the most sacred of metals. Use it as a protective talisman for the home, but be careful of the way it is hung. The horns pointing up means you are wise; the horns pointing down shows you are cautious; the horns pointing to the left means a witch...and the horns pointing to the right – a fool!

The other area of popular belief is the blacksmith's ability to cure certain ailments and the water in which the smith cooled hot metal had a curative reputation. Forge water, or 'thunder water' came from when the blacksmith was shoeing horses and he took the red-hot shoe out of the fire with pincers and dipped it in a barrel of water to cool it. The barrel would be there for always with the blacksmith using it every day and the water developing curative and magical properties. And hoof pairings obtained from the blacksmith were said to rid a dog of worms, hence there is always a dog in old paintings of the forge...

'Let Dogs Delight'

Dogs and humans became companions a long time ago and there is much written about them in superstition, folklore and animal husbandry: there was an old Welsh proverb that a man could be judged by the quality of his 'hawk and his hound'.

It is believed that dogs can sniff out evil, but superstitions surrounding them are usually ominous. When a dog howls in an otherwise silent night, it is said to be an omen of death, or at least of misfortune. A howling dog outside the house of a sick person was once thought to be an omen that they would die, especially if the dog was driven away and returned to howl again. A dog which gives a single howl, or three howls, and then falls silent is said to be marking a death that has just occurred nearby.

Dogs have always been credited with the power of sensing supernatural influences and being aware of the presence of ghosts; their barking, whimpering or howling is often the first warning of supernatural occurrences. A strange dog coming to the house means a new friendship; and to meet a spotted or black and white dog on your way to a business appointment is lucky. Three white dogs seen together are considered lucky in some areas; black dogs are generally considered unlucky, especially if they cross a traveller's path or follow someone and refuse to be driven away. The sight of a dog eating grass, rolling on the floor or scratching itself excessively are all said to be omens that rain is imminent.

Dogs were often used to cure other illnesses: one old charm used to cure children's ailments was to take some of the patient's hairs and feed them to a dog between slices of bread and butter – the ailment was believed to transfer to the animal, healing the patient. Another belief was to allow the family dog to lick a newborn baby to ensure that the person would be 'a quick healer'. One recipient of this treatment is now a colonel in the armed forces who does not appreciate his mother re-telling the story, but in his line of work it pays to be a 'quick healer'!

The old 'onion cure' for kennel cough is still resurrected on various websites, usually with the instruction to hang a net of onions in the kennel. The cure works, but the onions have to be bought locally (i.e. fresh); cut in half before being suspended along the whole kennel range and replaced every few days. This was a tried and tested remedy used by the big greyhound kennels of the past, but another instance of only knowing half a tale!

Wildlife and animal husbandry were integral parts of *The Secret People's* way of life because they had been brought up learning these customs from parents and grandparents who, themselves had been schooled in the ways of country folk by their parents and grandparents. It was to the countryman that village children took injured wildlife they'd found, and he either tended to the injury, or despatched the creature if the damage was too great.

Chapter Six

The Poacher

Once, the poacher was a man with big pockets in his raincoat sneaking on to an aristocrat's land to steal game. Now he is likely to be part of a gang from town, in it for hard cash, rampaging through the countryside with guns, crossbows or snares. Like the parish-pump witch, wise woman and cunning-folk, the old-fashioned poacher is a character who has faded from the rural community. Today's poaching is carried out as a commercial business with animals slaughtered on an epic scale so that wild life disappears from the fields and woodlands.

Like all people bred in the country, the labouring classes had always enjoyed a day's sport with a dog and gun, or ferret and nets, with the full approval of the landowner; rabbiting was as popular a village pastime as football is today. In 1831 saw changes to the Game Act and honest country folk were often driven by sheer necessity to turn poacher. The history of poaching goes back to the Forest Laws implemented by the feudal system that William of Normandy imposed on England after 1066; superseding the Anglo-Saxon laws in which rights to the forest (not necessarily just woods, but also heath, moorland, and wetlands) were not exclusive to the ruling classes, but were shared among the people. Feudal forest laws, in contrast, were harsh, forbidding not only the hunting of game within the forest, but even the cutting of wood or the collection of fallen timber, berries, or anything growing within the forest!

Back in the day, the poacher was a crafty thief who spent his time evading capture by the law while trying to catch his customary 'one for the pot' to feed himself and his family. According to E W Martin in *The Secret People*, he had a keen sense of natural beauty and a love of sport of its own sake; he was skilled in woodcraft, and intimately knew the woods, fields, hedges and trackways. 'In earlier days he risked life and liberty as he entered a wood at night, depending entirely on quickness of eye and readiness of mind, upon that sixth-sense tautness and awareness which was his only insurance against capture...'

Make no mistake about it, the punishments for poaching were extremely severe. Rural poverty continued to be widespread; wages were low and the labourers' diet was deplorable, so many turned to poaching merely to survive. To their neighbours, who often benefited from these night-time excursions, local poachers were viewed as heroes, with people rescuing poachers from the hands of keepers and police, and even intimidating those who took poachers to court.

As a counter-measure, the authorities introduced a variety of man-traps and spring-guns, the purpose of which was to kill, mutilate or break the poachers' legs. Poachers were sentenced to longer terms of imprisonment with the less fortunate being transported to places for fourteen years. Between 1750 and 1820, more poachers than before were hanged, particularly those convicted of using a firearm or wounding a gamekeeper. During 1830s the man-traps and spring-guns were made illegal, and an 1883 Act allowed tenants to kill rabbits and hares on their own farms, but the law still came down heavily on poachers, who could still be transported to penal colonies or imprisoned for up to seven years. The Poaching Prevention Act of 1862 said anyone suspected of carrying poaching 'implements' could be stopped and searched by the police, and poachers were treated more harshly than any other types of theft in the 19th century. Until the 20th century, most poaching was performed by impoverished people for subsistence purposes and to supplement their meagre diets.

In 1891, an old man known as 'Old Phil' published *The Confessions of a Poacher* and what is evident through the pages was his love of the open air and his feeling for nature. He'd learned the arts of his dubious profession from an old fowler, who taught him to understand the mysteries of the woods and coverts on a damp night.

He must know not only the land, but the ways of the game by heart. Every sign of wind and weather must be observed, as all help in the silent trade. Then there is the rise and the wane of the moon, the rain-bringing tides, and the shifting of the birds with the seasons. These and a hundred other things must be kept in an unwritten calendar, and only the poacher can keep it.

Nevertheless, even MP Richard Jefferies writing in 1878 recognised that the poacher had a 'spice of sneaking romance in his disposition – the Bohemian of the hamlet, whose grain of genius has sprouted under difficulties ... capable of touch which raises poaching into a fine art.' The poacher was undoubtedly one of *The Secret People*.

The Poacher's Dog

Stories concerning the poacher's dog have passed into rural legend with some incredible attributes accredited to these animals. On the bottom line, however, was the fact that by seizing the poacher's dog the police could identify the owner and so a whole collection of bar-room tales were told and re-told about lurchers running and hiding until the landowner or stranger passed. But, as one lurcher-man commented: 'Half the folk I've met who keep lurchers struggle with the recall command let alone the above!'

In *The Metropolitan Magazine*: 'Game, Game Laws & Poachers', an article written by a county magistrate in 1833, says:

After dusk the poacher affixes a net to the gate of a field, and then sends in his lurcher. This description of dog, who is really as much a poacher from instinct as his master is of a desire of gain, will traverse the whole field, even if it consists of twenty acres; and he will so work it, that if there be thirty hares in it, he will drive them all to the gate, where they are taken in the net... The sagacity of these dogs is most remarkable; they often hunt alone, and bring home the game to their masters.

A lurcher is a sight-hound (or long dog) crossed with a pastoral breed (herding group) or certain types of terrier. It is scarcely known outside Great Britain where it is highly prized by local countrymen for hunting rabbits, hares, game birds and even rats and foxes where they are considered pests. In the Middle Ages only royalty and nobility could own a purebred sight-hound (usually greyhounds or Scottish deerhounds). 'Crossbred puppies were unwanted except by the peasants, outlaws and gypsies, who trained the dogs to bring the kill home for the pot, often providing families with their only source of meat.'

Originally named the 'poacher's dog', the lurcher was prized for its speed, hunting ability, intelligence, tenacity and had great value to the poacher in its manner of hunting silently in the dark, never giving voice regardless of how many compelling noises and scents there were, and taking only the quarry that was indicated to him by his owner. Then he had to retrieve it live to hand, negotiating and clearing obstacles on his return, not to mention going home on command...obviously good lurchers were independent thinkers and highly trainable. The following extract reveals how a poacher felt about his dog:

> *I with my dogs went out one night,*
> *The moon shone clear and the stars gave light,*
> *O'er hedges, ditches, gates and rails,*
> *With my two dogs just at my heels,*
> *To catch a fat buck in Thorney Moor Fields*

One of the poacher's dogs returned lame and the poacher concluded that:

Some keeper has done this out of spite,
I will range the woods till I find that man,
I will tan his hide right well if I can.

This referred to the practice of deliberately laming a poacher's dog by chopping off three fore-claws; and described how keepers had the power to seize and kill hunting dogs. A good lurcher was a substantial investment; the dog may have been obtained with difficulty and from a distance, and its training – no less than that of a good sheep-dog – may have occupied months. Again and again the killing of dogs sparked off some act of protest or revenge.

Country Lore

The poacher was always well-versed in ways of the countryside and often wore another hat during daylight hours – working on the land. He would have a belief in the connection between the moon's cycle and living things on earth as reflected in the strict instructions to pay heed to the time for planting seeds and harvesting certain crops. For example: everything below ground (i.e. tubers, etc) on a waning moon; everything above ground (green vegetables) on a waxing moon. More specialised tasks, such as grafting fruit trees, were also ruled by the same principle. It had also been common knowledge for centuries that animals must be slaughtered during the waxing of the moon or the meat would be at best inferior and at worst downright bad.

There was also a long and barbarous tradition to kill the first creature of a certain species that was seen in the year. The usual reason for this was that one would overcome, or be free of, one's enemies for the coming year. It was also a widespread belief that when seeing the first young of certain species in the spring, it was lucky if they were facing you, but unlucky if you saw the tail first. This superstition applied to any domestic or farm animal, but was mostly said of lambs and foals.

The cuckoo's first call in spring still warrants annual reports in the correspondence columns of *The Times* and from early times the number of calls a cuckoo made indicated different things whether it applied to a young person (the time to marry), a married couple (the arrival of the next child) or old folk (how much longer they had to live). It was said that because the poor bird was kept so busy answering such enquiries, it had no time to build a nest and therefore had to offload its young onto foster-parents. Nonetheless, the cuckoo is considered to be a lucky bird and is widely believed that whatever state of health the listener is in at the time they hear the first call, so they will remain for the rest of the year. And a wish made at this time is supposed to come true.

Part of this arcane knowledge is recognising the presence of certain birds and animals in the vicinity and understanding their habits. Knowing that 'the moor-cock speeds into the background of brown peat and skims the contours of the heather-covered ground and is no easy target ...the woodcock's turns and twists through a hazel copse...a pigeon in flight never crosses directly over a man on open ground,' as wrote Ian Naill in *The New Poacher's Handbook*. 'When a far-away pigeon deviates in the line of flight you must learn to watch for the subsequent movement of sheep from the hedge to the corner of the field and the horse's pricked ears.'

The Secret People learn to interpret the language of Nature in all her guises and tell-tale tracks in the snow or mud show which animals or birds can also be found in the vicinity. A five-clawed imprint in the mud with a large bar-shaped pad shows that a badger passes that way on its nightly rounds and although quite numerous, these tracks are often the only sign that a set is nearby. A rabbit's skin taken cleanly off and the carcass consumed, a rabbit's burrow with a perpendicular hole dug down to it, or a wasps' nest cleaned out in the same way, all show a badger has been at work. Scattered piles of feathers and feathers looking like they've been cut diagonally with a hacksaw blade reveal a fox has caught its dinner. Similarly, a circle of feathers or a young bird lying with its body untouched but the flesh picked neatly from the neck and the head missing shows a sparrowhawk kill. A young pheasant without its head is an owl kill, while the same bird with only the brain missing reveals that the culprit is a jackdaw. A dead rabbit with a small hole in the neck announces the presence of a stoat.

The wild goose in flight over winter fields is a sight that stirs most people and these winter 'flightings' are an important part of country-lore. The birds come down from the Arctic for the milder weather and wreak havoc on the pastures. Geese are canny birds and have a roster of sentinels that keep watch and warn when danger is present; then they are in the air, yelping and conversing with each other as they look for another field or a roosting place far enough out in open water or exposed sands to keep them safe overnight. Their synchronised movements at dawn and dusk ensures that they arrive in their wintering area on almost the same day each autumn and depart in the same month each spring. They also provide the poacher with night cover since the call they make when flighting has an eerie, haunting sound and country people believed it to be made by the Cwm Annwn in Welsh; in England they were known as Gabriel hounds or wish hounds depending on the region. This yelping noise that the migrating geese make when they fly far overhead at night was said to be an omen of approaching death and would keep most folk abed at night.

Like old wives' tales, a great deal of country lore has a grain of truth behind it and as Ian Naill observes, these skills are not new. 'They are old, old like the scent of peat smoke from the lonely cottage; the cairn on the hill; the never-failing flight of the wild geese in October. Kindred spirits have studied these things...'

Poacher's Tricks

Anyone who has been acquainted with a local poacher will quickly realise how he manipulates the superstitions of his neighbours in order to keep them home abed while he has free range of the fields and woodland. Even those who know the vixen's sudden scream will feel the hairs on the back of the neck rise when the moon is half-shrouded and there is a hush over the countryside. It's not until the dog fox's answering bark makes it a duet that the unearthly sound is put back into perspective. Like the vixen, a stricken hare sounds like a human in extremis and it is not difficult to understand the belief that a witch took on a hare's form, only to be shot by a hunter. It was said that every hare that runs at twilight is likely to be bewitched; and to be sure a hare should be shot 'in the morning sun, on the long-shadowed fields at sunrise in autumn. Since witches, like bats, confine their activities to the half-light and no-one who wants to be sure of a hare should put up a gun at one when the light of day is fading.'

Despite the mixed reputation of the hare in folklore, they are consistently described as unlucky, unfit to eat, uncanny and witches in disguise. Poachers and shooters will kill a hare, but rarely would *The Secret People* ever take a dead animal into the home, because the hare is symbolic of the ancestral status it had in pre-Christian Britain. As one country woman remarked: 'My father wouldn't allow one in the house and although he loved game for the table, he'd never accept a hare. To him hares shouldn't be killed or eaten; they were sacrosanct. I never understood why he should think like that, but he did.'

The full moon of November is called the Poacher's Moon in England because it follows on after the great hunting season in October. The full moon extending into the quiet hours, especially when it coincides with clear skies, affords the poacher ideal conditions to mop up the luckless survivors for the winter game pot. Sometimes, however, the moon would be too full, the ground too hard and the night too still for venturing out.

The favourite markers for poachers were pieces of broken white crockery that remain visible however dark the night as they reflect any light there happens to be. He would mark a bush, rabbit holes and *smeuses* used by hares to help him set nets, or when ferreting by night. It's a poacher's trick worth remembering if wandering about the fields after dark.

To take a pheasant without any fuss, the birds were fed plum raisins soaked in rum; pheasants can't resist them and the drunken birds were easily despatched. A mixture of buckwheat and aniseed will have the same effect without making the birds drunk. Conversely, it's a trick of *The Secret People* to tempt pheasants into the garden to keep them safe from the guns.

To catch sight of a hare, another poacher's trick can be used by *The Secret People* for the sheer pleasure of watching the animal. Since they have a taste for blackthorn twigs, take a good, strong blackthorn stem, or one with plenty of twigs and stick it firmly in the ground in the open field. The smell of blackthorn will draw the hare to the spot and she will move around nibbling the twigs...but at the slightest movement or sound she'll be off.

It's always possible to discover whether ducks are regularly using a pond or any stretch of water by the evidence of preening feathers on the bank and the dibbled state of the mud at the edge. They like a nice shallow depth, at least on the edges, where they can up-end and search for food. All important to them is an easy sloping bank so that they can get in and out of the water without undue exertion. Ducks flight at dusk to their various feeding places, which are often ponds and backwaters and can provide endless entertainment especially when they have young.

October is the time to be on the look-out for rats moving into their winter quarters, especially in close proximity to dry stone walls and barns with their ancient wood piles and discarded bales of hay and straw. Watch for the tell-tale signs of 'grease trails' made by rats continuously dragging their tails along the same run. Even if there are no signs in the house, these trails will confirm that in the country we are never more than a few feet away from a rat. There is a charm for driving rats away simply by asking them, since they are said to respond well to civility. A time-honoured way of getting rid of them is to ask them politely to leave – either verbally, or written on a piece of paper which is put down their hole or pinned up nearby – using the following inscription:

R.A.T.S
A.R.S.T
T.S.R.A
S.T.A.R

Poaching has always been a dangerous occupation and it was easy to sustain some nasty injuries when out and about during the hours of darkness. Although often met with looks of horror, those thick cobwebs in the barn would staunch serious bleeding. Farmers still use this as an impromptu treatment for injured livestock because cobwebs have natural antiseptic and antifungal properties that help keep wounds clean and free of infection. In traditional European medicine, cobwebs were used on wounds and cuts to help healing and reduce bleeding. The reason they heal so well and so quickly is because cobwebs are rich in vitamin K – the clotting vitamin. The web itself is a biologically neutral material so the silk will not cause an infection as long as clean webs are used, although some remedies say the blacker and thicker the web, the better it served. For example, after a battle, the ancient Greeks would apply vinegar to irrigate wounds, pour honey into them and then use cobwebs to keep the honey in the wounds. The web itself is incredibly strong and a ball of it stuffed into an open wound or used to cover an open wound will dry out and harden over time; but is easily removed with the use of a little hot water.

Similarly, the application of a dock leaf to ease nettle stings has been used for at least 650 years and many country people are still convinced that docks and nettles always grow in close proximity for human convenience. It was necessary to recite a charm to make the remedy work: *'Nettle in, dock out/Dock in/nettle out/Nettle in, dock out/Dock rub nettle out'* – a rhyme that was in use in Chaucer's time. Other aspects of nettle lore include the plant being eaten when young as a vegetable, and for the treatment of a wide variety of ailments.

Ian Nail continues: 'The net is no new device, the yelp of the fox no new sound... There is an old look in the eye of the ragged barnyard cockerel, a strange wisdom in the crow, and the same timelessness and natural movement in the way of a tall-legged hare passing through a hill of gorse... These things were there when man began to learn his cunning...' It was the poacher who taught local children woodcraft and fieldcraft that was nothing like the 'nature study' that was taught in school.

Weather Lore

The Secret People keep a keen eye on the weather since it was pointless going out if the weather was about to change and the rabbits stayed in the warren. The following are a handful of the sayings and rhymes that are part and parcel of our native weather lore – some of which have turned out to be reliable omens since many of them originated within the depths of the countryside:

January: Usually the coldest month of the year and there's a country saying that *'as the days lengthen, the cold strengthens'*. For those who pay attention to weather lore, frost and snow are not unwelcome sights at this time – in fact, mild weather during any of the winter months (especially January) is a bad omen.

February: Renowned for having the most unpleasant weather of the year, although farmers welcome the rain and snow because it prepares the ground for sowing and germination of the seed. *'If in February there be no rain, 'tis neither good for hay nor grain.'*

March: In this month the countryside begins its transition from brown to green, with windy and dry weather generally considered to be a good thing: *'March winds and April showers bring forth May flowers.'*

April: Known for the unpredictability and changeability of its weather: *'April weather, rain and sunshine both together.'* The proverbial 'April showers' are welcomed by farmer and gardener alike, but the blossoming of the blackthorn towards the end of the month is often accompanied by a period of unseasonably cold weather – hence a blackthorn winter.

May: Prolonged spells of warm weather in May are a welcome foretaste of summer, but it is dangerous to assume that winter is past and gone. Every child knows that red skies are said to be omens of forthcoming weather: *'Red sky at night, shepherd's delight, Red sky in the morning, shepherd's warning.'*

June: Warm dry weather in June is ideal, but crops need rain for growth, as well as sun for ripening and this month sees the start of the season for summer storms. In British country-lore the oak tree has long had the reputation of being a safe place to shelter during a thunderstorm although there is the popular rhyme that disagrees: *'Beware of the oak; it draws the stroke.'*

July: Although July is one of the hottest months of the year, weather lore seems to be preoccupied with rain: *'If the first day of July be rainy weather 'twill rain more or less for four weeks together.'*

August: The hottest days of the year often fall in the month of August, but farmers welcome such weather. It may, however, warn of a hard winter to come: *'If the first week of August be warm, the winter will be long and white.'*

September: Everyone hopes for temperate weather in September, so that crops will not be damaged before they can be gathered in: *'September blow soft, till fruit be in the loft,'* while the three days preceding the Autumnal Equinox are supposed to determine the weather for the following three months.

October: St Simon and St Jude's Day (28th October) traditionally marks the end of fine weather and the commencement of gales and storms, hence the saying: *'A good October and a good blast to blow the hog acorns and mast.'*

November: There are many regional variations on: *'If the ice in November will bear a duck then all the rest will be slush and muck,'* or, *'A cold November means a mild, wet winter.'*

December: The traditional December weather as depicted in paintings and Victorian pictures, with frozen ponds and deep snow, is no longer an annual occurrence in much of Britain, and on the 31st attention turns to the direction of the wind:

> *If New Year's Eve night the wind blow south,*
> *It betokeneth warmth and growth;*
> *If west, much milk and fish in the sea;*
> *If north, much cold and storms there will be;*
> *If east, the trees will bear much fruit;*
> *If north-east, flee it, man and brute.*

Animals and plants play an important part in forecasting the weather, and it was a country belief that pigs can 'see the wind' and that bad weather could be predicted from watching pigs' behaviour. They were said to behave in a peculiar fashion before and during a storm, which may be because they are sensitive to atmospheric changes. The most reliable sign, however, is the scarlet pimpernel that is also known as the 'ploughman's weather glass' since its petals forecast whether it will be wet or fine.

In truth, however, the poacher foretold the weather by looking at the sky with its various cloud formations and the wind velocity...and could often smell if rain was on the way. Knowledge of the weather played an important part in the poaching tradition, the craft of men who knew and loved the countryside and invoked unorthodox skills to catch their game, which they took sparingly, as they needed it.

One for the Pot

A poacher's larder would have been a meagre one, and although fewer people eat wild rabbit meat since the days of 'the plague' and not all guns are skilful enough to bring down a pigeon in flight, both formed part of the weekly diet for most country people. The plentiful supply of pigeons and pheasants still plays an important part in rural kitchens and roast pheasant and pigeon breasts make a pleasant change to normal fare. The following recipes were adapted for *Traditional Witchcraft for Field and Hedgerow* since most of the poacher's meals would probably have been cooked in the frying pan!

Recipe for Pheasant Breasts

Coat the breasts with egg and breadcrumbs. Lay them flat in a buttered pan. Add a few drops of lemon juice; cover the pan and cook for six to eight minutes over a very hot heat. Cooking must be extremely rapid and done without boiling; the liquid being limited to the few drops of lemon juice. Place on a warm dish and garnish with a green vegetable tossed in butter.

Pigeon Breast Casserole

Breasts from four pigeons

2oz butter

3 slices lean bacon, chopped

8 spring onions, trimmed and chopped

8oz button mushrooms, wiped clean and halved

1 pint water

4 teaspoons tomato puree

Grated rind of lemon

In a large frying pan, melt the butter and when the foam subsides add the bacon and spring onions and cook until the bacon is lightly browned. Remove from the pan and place in a large ovenproof casserole. Place the pigeon breasts in the frying pan and cook them, turning frequently until they are lightly browned. Transfer to the casserole. Add the mushrooms to the pan and cook for about 3 mins or until they are well coated with butter. Tip the contents of the pan over the meat. Return the pan to the heat, pour in the water and stir in the tomato purée and lemon rind. When the liquid boils, remove the pan from the heat and pour contents into the casserole. Cover and place in the oven for 1 hour or until the breasts are tender when pierced with the point of a sharp knife (350F, 180C, Mark 4). Remove casserole from the oven and serve immediately.

Game Soup

2 pints game stock from carcasses of 2 game birds

1 onion

1 carrot

1 stick celery

2oz butter

1 bay leaf

Salt and pepper

1oz butter
1oz plain flour
1 teaspoons redcurrant jelly
2 teaspoons lemon juice
2 tablespoons sherry or red wine

Peel and chop the onion, scrub and chop the carrot, wash and slice the celery. Melt the butter in a large pan and lightly fry the vegetables, turning them in the hot fat until lightly browned. Add stock, bay leaf, salt and pepper, and simmer for 1 hour. Finely chop any meat picked from the carcasses. Melt butter, stir in flour and fry until light brown. Strain the soup and gradually stir in the butter mixture. Bring to the boil and cook for 2-3 minutes. Add the meat and reheat. Add the redcurrant jelly, lemon juice and sherry or red wine. Reheat and serve at once.

Farmhouse Scramble

3 eggs
3oz cooked ham
Mustard to taste
½ gill milk
1oz butter
6oz cooked potatoes
1 tblsp chopped Jack-by-the-hedge (wild garlic)

Beat the eggs in a basin. Add the milk. Rub the potatoes through a fine sieve and stir into the beaten egg mix. Add the ham, finely minced, the Jack-by-the-hedge, and the mustard to taste. Melt the butter in a frying pan. Pour in the mixture. As it begins to set, let the liquid run below the edges and cook until the whole is set.

Farmhouse Curry
Left-over meat
1 tablespoon apple chutney
1 dessertspoon curry powder
2 tablespoons milk
1 tablespoon flour
1 apple
1 onion
2oz butter
1 pint stock

Chop the meat finely. Melt the fat and when smoking hot fry the onion, flour, and curry powder together for a few moments, stirring all the time. Add the chopped apple, salt to taste, and stock. Stir constantly until the sauce is smooth and boiling, then remove the pan to the side of the fire. Cover and simmer for ½ hour. Add the chopped meat. Thin to taste with a little milk. Stir in apple chutney and bring to the boil again. Add a few drops of lemon juice and milk. Serve at once on a hot dish with boiled rice.

Harvest Pudding
1 packet sage and onion stuffing
2oz grated cheese
4oz cooked ham, chopped
2 large eggs, separated
Black pepper
Pinch of mustard powder

Prepare the packet of sage and onion stuffing as indicated on the packet and allow to cool. Stir in cheese, ham, egg-yolks, some freshly ground black pepper and the mustard powder. Mix well. Beat the egg whites until stiff and fold them in lightly with a metal spoon. Turn the mixture into a greased ovenproof dish and bake in a moderate oven, Gas 5 (375F/190C) for 35 minutes. Serve with lightly cooked green vegetables, potatoes or a green salad.

The Secret People know that some fields produce a better crop of mushrooms than others and most have their own 'secret' places that they harvest year after year. It was always considered necessary to pick the area bare so that any later-comers wouldn't find a single mushroom! The poacher would be picking his share on the way home at dawn – especially looking for the great horse mushrooms that stain the gravy black – and enjoying a feast that is tastier than any commercial growers can provide. With egg and bacon this would have been considered a dish for a king.

Back in the day there was 'hardly a country parish in rural Britain without a lake, pond, stream, meandering or turbulent river in which fish of one aspect or another are found,' mused Ian Niall in *English Country Traditions*. 'And when times were poor, any kind of fish, muddy-tasting or not, were welcome on the countryman's table.' And wildfowling, although a dangerous pastime, has always been in a class of its own and not governed by the land-laws that outlawed poaching. Below the high watermark of the East Anglian or Romney marshes, the common man could bag himself a migrating duck, wigeon or goose without fear of reprisal, and often bag enough to be shipped to the game merchants in London. It was a seasonal trade and meant stalking through icy reeds and frozen pools, or paddling a skiff through the mist in treacherous waters.

Historically, the parish-pump witch and wise woman had much in common with the poacher since all their activities could be deemed illegal, and the Witchcraft Act wasn't repealed until 1951, when it was replaced with the Fraudulent Mediums Act in 1954. And a final point to ponder: since the 1980s, the term 'poaching' has also referred to the illegal

harvesting of wild plant species, which means that many of *The Secret People* could still be breaking the law!

Chapter Seven

The Church Calendar

Most of the holy days in the pagan and Christian calendars were fixed and celebrated on the same day every year. Other sacred or festival days were movable and changed every year as the equinoxes and solstices varied; while many of the traditions and customs practised on holy days can be traced back to pre-Christian times when specific locations were endowed with magical or spiritual attributes that were incorporated into festivals and celebrations. These customs were so firmly established in the hearts and minds of the people, that when Christianity was finding a foothold in Britain, the Church of Rome integrated and sanctified them. The Church slowly drew the people in by allowing the old festivals to continue with a coat of Christianity overlaid upon them. The magical powers believed to be associated with specific people, things and places were transferred, and their powers then attributed to God and his saints.

The following are the medieval saints and feast days as they would have been celebrated in the 14th century (taken from the calendars compiled by the Medieval Combat Society and the blog La Bella Donna: The Italian Renaissance ReLived). Although many of the 'saints' originally belonged to pagan (including Roman and Celtic) folklore, they were adopted by the Church and their 'histories' rewritten; many being imported 'saints' from mainland Europe, who were holy people and ordinary folk who lived extraordinary lives. St Augustine ordered that none of the pagan sites of worship in Britain were to be destroyed, but instead turned into Christian churches, so the people would continue to use the indigenous holy places sacred to the Old Gods, and rename them for new saints introduced into the

Church calendar by Rome.

Wells and springs were venerated by pagans and it was thought necessary to propitiate the guardians by ritually adorning the source of fresh water with garlands and greenery. Once Christianity became established, these pagan practices were deplored and forbidden, but the custom was so deeply entrenched that the Church turned pagan springs into holy wells and the custom of well-dressing continues to the present day – dedicated to one saint or another. Nevertheless, the 'old parish churches retained the mysterious quality of an ancient sacred place which has never been out of the possession of a long line of simple rural people,' wrote Ronald Blythe in *Akenfield*.

A considerable amount of healing and spell-casting was carried out in saints' names and the majority of *The Secret People* would be in regular attendance at a local church, which also provided a gathering place for the community. The Church calendar would be the only method of reckoning available to the common people and was calculated according to the old Julian calendar on which many traditional British customs were originally based. The festivals marked in bold are the 'hidden' observances of earlier pagan customs, superstitions and celebrations. The early liturgical calendar, like its earlier Roman counterpart, was also based on the agricultural year and so some of these celebrations have also been added to contrast with the Christian feast days.

The Old Calendar

In 325AD the Nicene council officially adopted the 'Julian calendar', which declared that a year would be 365 days and 6 hours long with March 25th marking the New Year. Many centuries passed until astronomers discovered the flaw in the Julian calendar, which exceeded the newly measured solar year by 11 minutes. From 325AD to 1582AD, this amounted to a difference of nearly 10 days! In order to correct this error Pope

Gregory XIII ordered a new calendar, named as the 'Gregorian calendar', and the difference of 11 days had to be cut down.

Those missing days – 3rd to 13th September 1582 – simply disappeared, but it helps to explain some of the anomalies in dating between many of the ancient festivals and the current calendar, which should always be taken into account when researching calendar customs and other popular festivals. For many years Britain retained its own internal 'Old Style' dates, and so there were often two of each festival every year – for example Christmas Day and Old Christmas Day eleven days later.

January

01: **Month named for** *Januarius,* **the ancient Italian divinity and sun-god, represented with two faces looking in front and behind. The Anglo-Saxons called it** *Wolfmonath,* **when wolves moved closer to human habitation to feed off the carcases of fallen stock.** St Maelrhys; St Elvan and St Mydwyn (2nd century); Circumcision, The Solemnity of Mary. New Year's Day. **Feast day of** *Strenia,* **the old Sabine goddess of good health, and in her names gifts were exchanged for good luck.**

02: St Basil the Great of Aix, France (c329-379), patron of hospital administrators and reformers; St Gregory of Nazianzen (c329-389) patron of harvests and poets.

03: St Genevieve, patron saint of Paris (c422-512); St Baise, patron of wool-combers and invoked against throat ailments. **Feast Day of** *Pax,* **Roman goddess of peace.**

04: St Simeon the Stylite (c390-459).

05: St Julien; St Edward the Confessor; Vigil of Epiphany, **Wassail;** *Lars Compitalia,* **festival of the Roman guardians of the crossroads celebrated with socialising and entertaining.**

06: St Peter of Canterbury (d607); St Hywyn (Ewwn, Owen) of Aberdaron Gwynedd, Wales (d516); Epiphany; **Plough**

Monday is the first Monday after Epiphany when men were supposed to get back to work on the land. Twelfth Night.

07: St Raymond of Pennafort (1175-1275); St Brannock of Braunton; **St Distaff's Day when women resumed their household work after Christmas.**

08: St Wulsin of Westminster (d1002).

09: St Adrian of Canterbury (d709); St Brihtwald (Berhtwald, Beorhtweald, Brihtwald) of Canterbury (d731); **St Fillan – known for his holy well at Loch Katrine in Scotland that bestowed fertility.**

10: St Paul (d342); Geraint of Wales (9th century).

11: St Egwin of Worcester; St Brandan of Ireland (5th century); *Carmentalia,* **first feast day of the Roman goddess of prophecy and childbirth; Feast of** *Juturna,* **Roman goddess of fountains and a goddess of the underworld whose symbol is a spring. An ancient fire festival celebrated as Old New Year's Eve after the calendar reforms.**

12: St Benedict Biscop of Wearmouth (d690).

13: St Hilary (Hilarii) of Poitiers (d368), **St Hilary's Day was said to be the coldest day of the year and after whom the 'Hilary term' in some universities and law courts is named.** St Erbin (Ervan, Ernie, Erbyn, Hermes) of Cornwall and Devon (5th century); St Kentigern Mungo of Scotland (d603); St Elian of Cornwall, (6th century).

14: St Felix of Nola (d260); St Kentigern (c516-601); St Deusdedit of Canterbury (d664).

15: St Ita (Deirdre and Mida) (d570); St Blaithmaic of Ireland (d823); St Ceowulf of Northumbria (d764).

16: St Honoratus of Aries, France (350-429); St Henry of Cocket Northumbria (d1127).

17: St Antony of Egypt (251-356) the patron of domestic animals; St Milburga of Wenlock (d715); *Felicitas,* **the Roman personification of good fortune, happiness or felicity.**

18: St Volusian of Tours (d496); St Ulfrid of England (d1028); St

Day of Cornwall.

19: St Canutus of Denmark (Canute IV, Knud) (d1086); **St Wulstan (Wulfstan) of Worcester (1008-1095) – famed for his healing and prophetic abilities;** St Branwallader of Jersey (6th century).

20: St Fabian (d250); **St Agnes Day Eve when girls would perform certain rituals before going to bed to reveal who their future husband was to be. St Agnes was the patron of virgins.**

21: St Agnes of Rome (d305).

22: St Paschasius of Vienne, France (d312); St Brithwald of Ramsbury (d1045); **Feast of St Vincent. The weather on St Vincent's Day is used to forecast the weather: wind and sun are favourable omens for the coming year's crops and grain.**

23: St Paul's Day; St Ormond of St Maire (6th century).

24: St Bertrand of Saint-Quentin (7th century); St Cadoc (Docus, Cathmael, Cadfael) (d580); *Paganalia,* **a Roman celebration of sowing and associated with the earth-goddess Ceres.**

25: St Amarinus of Clermont, France (d676); St Dwynwen of Brecknock; St Eochod (d697); St Dwynwen of Wales; *Paganalia* **and the Feast of Bacchus for the protection of seed from birds.**

26: St Eystein (d1168); St Margaret (1243-1271); St Alberic (d1109); St Paula (d404); St Robert of Newmister (1100-1159); St Conan (d648); St Thordgith (Theoregitha) of Barking, England (d960).

27: St Emerius (8th century); St Gamo of Bretigny, France (8th century); St Gilduin of Dol (d1077); St Julian of Le Mans (3rd century).

28: St Cannera of Bantry, Ireland (d530); St Antilnus of Brantome, France (8th century); St Thomas Aquinas (1226-1274).

29: St Gildas the Wise (d576); St Blath (d523); St Voloc (d724).

30: St Aidan of Connaught (Edan, Modoc, Maedoc) (d626); St Adamnan of Coldingham (d680); St Madoes.

31: St Aedh (Aiden) of Ferns; **Roman festival of Hecate in her**

form as queen of ghosts and magic.

February

01: Month named *Februarius*, the 'month of expiation', taken from the Sabine word februm, meaning a purgative. St Bridgit, Brigid, Bride. Daughter of the Dagda and one of the Tuatha Dé Danann. She is considered the patroness of poetry, smithing, medicine, arts and crafts, cattle and other livestock, sacred wells, serpents (in Scotland) and the arrival of early spring. The original Anglo-Saxon name for the month was 'Sprout-kale' for the vegetable that began to sprout at this time. It was also referred to as *Solmonath* or 'cake month' because cakes and other offerings were presented to the gods; St Ignatius; St Crewanna of Crowan (5th century); *Februm*, sacred to Juno Februra and a month during which reverence was shown to the spirits of the ancestors and the rebirth of spring.

02: St Lawrence of Canterbury (d 619); St Freock of Cornwall, England; Purification of Our Lady Mary, the Presentation of the Lord; **Imbolc. Candlemas.**

03: St Blase (Blaise), patron of the wool industry (d316); St Margaret of England, patron of the dying; St Werburga of Mercia (d785).

04: St Gilbert of Sempringham (c1083-1189); St Modan (6th century); St Aldate of Gloucester (d600); *Fornicalia*, **a Roman spring corn festival celebrated in the honour of the goddess, Fornax.**

05: St Agatha the virgin, patron of nurses (d251).

06: St Dorothy (Dorothea), patron of gardeners and flowers (c313); St Amand of Poitou, patron of wine makers, brewers and innkeepers, (584-676).

07: St Richard of Wessex; St Tressan (d550); St Augulus of London (d303); *Favonius* – **the Roman festival of spring sowing.**

08: St Elfleda of Whitby (Edifleda, Elfeda, Elgiva, or Ethelfieda) (d714); St Cuthman of Steyning, Sussex, patron of shepherds (d900).

09: St Apollonia, patron of dentistry (d249); St Eingan of Cumberland (6th century).

10: St Scholastica of Plombaria (d543); St Trumwin of Whitby (d704).

11: St Benedict of Anian (c750-821); St Severinus (6th century).

12: St Julian, patron of carnival workers, ferrymen, hospitallers, innkeepers, knights, murderers, pilgrims and shepherds; St Ethelwald of Lindisfarne.

13: St Ermengild of Ely (d700); St Dyfnog of Wales; St Huno of Ely (d690); St Lezin of Angers (7th century). *Faunalia*, **Roman festival of Faunus, guardian of crops and herds.**

14: St Cyril and Methodius (9th century); **St Valentine was originally a pagan priest in 3rd century Rome and is now the patron of lovers.**

15: St Sigfrid of Sweden (d1045); St Quinidius of Vaison, France (d579); St Dochow of Cornwall (d473); **Roman** *Lupercalia* **honouring the gods of fertility, woodlands and pasture.**

16: St Onesimus (d90); St Gilbert of Sempringham (12th century).

17: St Loman (d450); St Finan of Lindisfarne (d661).

18: St Simeon (Simon) (d106); St Angibert of Saint-Riquier, Picardy (d814); St Colman of Lindisfarne (d676); *Quirinalia* **is a festival to honour Qurinus a Roman/Sabine deity – possibly a war god; also known as** *Stultorum Feriae*, **or Feast of Fools.**

19: St Odran (d452); St Valerius of Antibes (d450).

20: St Wulfric of Compton, England (d1154), a seer with the gifts of prophecy and healing, who became known as a healer of body, mind and spirit for all those who sought him out; St Eleutherius of Tournai (d532).

21: St Peter Damian (c988-1072); St Avitus II of Clermont, France (d689); St Felix of Metz (2nd century).

22: St Margaret of Cortona (1247-1297), patron of the falsely accused, homeless and insane; St Elwin (6th century); St Raynerius of Beaulieu, France (d967).

23: St Polycarp of Smyrna (d156); St Oswald of Worcester; St Boswell of Melrose (d661); St Jurmin of East Anglia, (7th century); **St Milburga of Wenlock (d 715) loved flowers, birds (over which she had a mysterious power), country life, and country people, to sit and work in the sun and tend the herbs in her garden, and to visit the villages nearby. People came to her with their troubles and ailments and even ascribed to her miraculous cures. Milburga was venerated for her humility, holiness, the miracles she performed, and for the gift of levitation she is said to have possessed.** *Terminalia* **was held to be the last day of the Roman sacred year.**

24: St Pretextatus (6th century); Leap day (February 24 occurred twice); **St Wallburgha's Eve, when it was believed witches and evil spirits were abroad.** St Matthias's Day – St Matthew as known as thirteenth Apostle – **according to various weather proverbs, a frost on St Matthias's Day will last for anything from a week to two months.**

25: St Ethelbert of Kent (d616); St Wallburgha of Devon, (710-779).

26: St Porphyrius (c353-420); St Victor of Champagne, (d995); St Robert of Newmister, Northumberland, (1000-1159).

27: St Baldomerus of Lyons (d650).

28: St Oswald (d992), patron of soldiers; St Romanus of Condat (d460); St Ruellinus of Treguier, Brittany (6th century).

29: (See 24th February) St Cassian (c360-433).

Leap years presented a problem for the calendar of saints' days. In the ancient Roman calendar introduced by Julius Caesar, which was the basis of the medieval calendar, the extra day in a leap year was inserted as the second sixth day' before the Kalends of March – that is, the day after the 23rd day of February. This continued as a general practice in the Middle Ages. The day inserted after the 23rd was empty of saints, so the Feast of Matthew was moved from what, in a leap year, would be the 25th of February to fill the blank created by Leap Day (the 24th).

March

01: Known as *Martius* for the god of war and fabled father of Romulus. The Norsemen regarded the month as 'the lengthening month that wakes the alder and blooms the whin (gorse)' calling it *Lenct* – meaning Spring. It was a period of enforced fasting when winter stores were running low and as such was incorporated into the Church calendar and renamed Lent. The Anglo-Saxons referred to it as *Lenetmonath;* St David of Menevia, patron of Wales (d544); St Albinus of Tincillocof Brittany (d550); **St David's Day.**

02: St Chad of Lichfield, patron of astronomers (d673). **Originally the Feast of Ceadda, a Celtic deity associated with sacred springs and wells;** St Cynibild (7th century); St Fergna of Iona (d637).

03: St Cunegundes (Kunegunde) (d1040); St Winwaloe (Winnal, Wonnow, Wynwallow, and Gwenno, Winwalloc) (6th century); St Cele-Christ of Leinster (d728).

04: St Owen of Lastingham (d680).

05: St Piran of Padstow, Cornwall; St Caron of Tregaron; St Kieran of Ossory, Ireland.

06: St Bilfrid of Lindisfarne (8th century); St Cadroe (d 976); St Kyneburga, Kyneswide and Tibba of Mercia (d680); St Balther of Lindisfarne (d756).

07: Sts Perpetua and Felicitas watch over all mothers and children who are separated from each other because of war or persecution (d203); St Ardo of Aachen (d843); St Esterwine of Wearmouth (d668).

08: St Felix of Dunwich, Suffolk; St Beoadh of Ardcarne, Ireland (d518).

09: St Bosa of York (d705); St Gregory of Nyssa (c330-395).

10: St Kessag of Cashel, Ireland (d560); **Kessog was Scotland's patron saint before Saint Andrew, and his name was used as a battle cry by the Scots; depicted in a soldier's habit, holding a bent bow with an arrow in it.**

11: St Sophronius (7th century); St Constantine of Cornwall.

12: St Maximilian, patron of families, prisoners and journalists (d295); St Theophanes (d968); St Alphege of Winchester (d951).

13: St Euphrasia, a patron of travellers (380-410).

14: St Maud (Mathildis) d.968); St Boniface Curitan of Ross, Scotland (d660); *Equiria Mamurius* – **originally the first full moon of the new year – when an old man dressed in goatskins was ceremoniously banished from the city.**

15: St Zacharias, patron of expectant mothers (d752); **the famous 'Ides of March' linked to the death of Julius Ceasar, and the festival of *Anna Perenna* (originally) the full moon in what was then the first month of the year). She was the goddess of the circle of the year, or 'she who begins and ends the year'.**

16: St Abraham (d360).

17: St Joseph of Arimathea (1st century); St Patrick of Kilpatrick, Ireland (d464); **St Patrick's Day (Ireland); *Liberalia* was celebrated in Rome in honour of the god of the vine as a great carnival; it was at this festival that Roman youths first assumed the toga virilise, or 'manly gown'.**

18: St Cyril of Jerusalem (c315-386); St Edward the Martyr of England (c962-979).

19: St Joseph of Nazareth (1st century); *Quinquatria* **and** *Minervalia*, **festivals of Mars and Minerva that culminated in great processions and banquets.**

20: St Cuthbert of Lindisfarne (d687), patron of northern England; St Herbert of Derwentwater (d687); St Wulfran (d720).

21: St Basil of Ancyra (d362); St Enda of Ireland; **Spring Equinox – Eostra Anglo-Saxon goddess of spring.**

22: St Ludger (743-809); St Trien of Killelga, Ireland (5th century).

23: St Tutilo (d915); St Ethelwald (Odilwald) of Fame Island,

England.

24: St Rupert (d710); St Macartan of Clogher, Ireland; St Hildelitba (Hildilid, Hideltha) of Barking (d712).

25: St Zosimus of Syracuse (d660); St Dismas, patron of those condemned to death; St Harold of Gloucester, England (d1168); St Robert of Bury St Edmunds (d1181**); start of the year in England until the adoption of the Gregorian Calendar in 1752;** Annunciation of the Blessed Virgin Mary. Lady Day. *Hilaria* **was a Roman festival of joy in honour of the goddess Cybele, that ended a nine-day period of fasting.**

26: St Alfwold of Sherborne (d1058); William of Norwich (d1144); **St Govan – known for his healing well in Wales.**

27: St Alkeld (Athilda) of Yorkshire, (10th **century) of the holy well at Middleham.**

29: St Berthold of Limoges (d1195); St Mark, patron of lawyers.

30: St Osburga of Coventry (d1018).

31: St Felicis watches over parents who have lost a child in death; martyrs; sterility and widows; St Dominic, patron of astronomers and founder of the Inquisition.

Hocktide: A very old mediaeval festival used to denote the Monday and Tuesday in the week following the second Tuesday after Easter. Together with Whitsuntide, the twelve days of Yuletide and the week following Easter marked the only vacations of the husbandman's year during slack times in the cycle of the seasons.

April

01: Named *Aprilius* **by the Romans to mean 'the opening thing' – the month of April during which the earth opens itself to fertility. The Anglo-Saxon called this time** *Eosturmonath* **or 'Goddessmonth';** St Hugh of Greoble (1053-1132); St Walerics of Leuconay, France (d622); St Cellach of Iona (9**th **century);** *Veneralis,* **the Feast of Venus and All Fool's Day for the Romans when everyone participated in**

ludricrous celebrations.

02: St Basil patron of hospital workers (329-379); St Mary of Egypt (c355-431).

03: St Agape of Evoriacum (d304); St Richard of Chichester (1197-1253).

04: St Isidore of Seville (d636); St Guier (Gwerir) of Cornwall.

05: St Becan of Kill-Beggan, Westmeath (6th century); St Derferl-Gadarn of Lianderfel, Gwynedd (5th or 6th century); St Ethelburga of Northumbria (d647).

06: St William of Eskill (c1125-1203); St Brychan of Wales; St Ulehad of Anglesey; St Elstan of Winchester (d981).

07: St Brynach of Carn-Englyi, Gwynedd (5th century); St Goran (Woronus) of Bodmin (6th century).

08: St Dionysius of Corinth (d171); St Aedesius (d306).

09: St Waldetrudis (Waudru) (7th century); St Madrun; St Hedda of Peterborough (d870); Martyrs of Croyland.

10: St Fulbert (d1029); St Beocca of Surrey (d870); St Malchus of Ireland.

11: St Guthlac (c673-714); St Stanislas (1030-1079); St Machai of Bute.

12: St Zeno, patron of fishermen and anglers (d380); St Wigbert (d690).

13: St Caradoc of Wales (d1124); St Gunioc of Scotland (d838).

14: St Lambert of Lyon (d688).

15: St Paternus of Wales (5th century); St Ruadan of Ireland (d584); *Fordicidia*, **a Roman festival to promote the fertility of cattle and fields.**

16: St Magnus of Orkney (1075-1116); St Padarn; St Drogo of Sebourg, France (d1186).

17: St Stephen, patron of horses (d1134).

18: St Cogitosus of Kildare, Ireland (8th century); St Gebuinus of Lyons (d1080).

19: St Elphege (Alphege) of Canterbury (953-1012).

20: St Agnes of Montpulciano (c1274-1317).

21: St Anselm of Canterbury (c1033-1109); St Beuno of Clynnog, Carnarvonshire (6th century); *Parilia*, **a festival to honour the old Roman pastoral goddess Pales and observed by driving livestock through burning straw.**

22: St Theodore of Sykeon (d613); St Arwald of the Isle of Wight (d686); St Authaire of La-Feste-sur-Jouarre, France (7th century).

23: St George (c303); St Felix of Vienne, France (d212); **St George's Day (England).**

24: St Mellitus of London (d624); St Egbert of Lindisfarne (8th century); St Mark's Eve.

25: St Mark the Evangelist (1st century); **Cuckoo Day celebrates the return of the cuckoo each year to guarantee good weather.**

26: St Riquier of Celles, France (d645).

27: St Zita (1212-1272); St Enoder (Cnydr, Keneder, Quidic) of Wales (6th century); St Winewald of Beverley (d731); *Floralia*: **beginning of a Roman spring festival that honoured Flora the goddess of flowers.**

28: St Cronan of Roscrea (d626).

29: St Hugh of Cluny (1024-1109); St Edmund, the original patron saint of England (see 20th November); St Endellion of Cornwall (6th century); St Ava of Dinart; St Wilfred the Younger of York (d744).

30: St Erconwald of London; St Adjutor of Vernonsur-Seine (d1131); St Cynwal of Wales (6th century); **Beltaine Eve; Walpurgis Night.**

May

01: Named for *Maia*, a local Italian goddess, wife of Mars and mother of Mercury. The Anglo-Saxon name for the month was *Trimilki*, meaning 'three-milk' because in that month they began to milk their kine three times a day and signifying a time of plenty. St Philip, patron of hatters and pastry chefs and St James, patron of apothecaries; St Asaph of Wales (d600); St Brieuc of Wales (d510); **May Day celebrations.**

02: St Athanasius of Alexandra (c296-373); St Ultan of Burgh Castle; **Continuance of *Floralia*, a Roman festival which honoured Flora, goddess of flowers.**

03: St Philip (1st century); St James the Less, patron of hat makers (d62); St Gluvias (Glywys) of Cornwall (6th century); St Ethelwin of Lindsey (8th century); St Ethelred of Bardney; **Roodmass – this ritual is along the lines of the *Quem Quæritas Trope*, the oldest-known recorded mystery play, which was usually performed right before Easter Mass. Quotes from Malory's *Morte d'Arthur* feature fairly prominently. Roodmas (the English name for Beltaine, as in the set with Candlemas, Lammas, and Hallowmas) should be performed as near 1st May as is practical – see 14th September.**

04: Veneration of the Thorn; St Monica, patron of married women, abuse victims, alcoholics, alcoholism and difficult marriages.

05: St Hilary protector against snake bites (c401-459); St Eadbert of Lindisfarne; St Hydroc of Lanhydroc, Cornwall (5th century); St Echa of Crayk, England (d767).

06: St Petronax (d747); St Eadbert (Edbert) of Lindisfarne (d698).

07: St John of Beverley (d721); St Liudhard (Liphard, Letard) of Canterbury (d600).

08: St Peter, patron of fishermen, net makers, and ship builders (d1174); Vigil of the Assumption. **Festival of the Helston Furry Dance that is said to be one of the oldest examples of a communal spring festival dance.**

09: St Pachomius (c292-348); Christopher of Lycea, patron of travellers; *Lemuria* **were the odd-numbered days between 9th-11th May when domestic ceremonies were performed in honour of the ancestors.**

10: St Bede, patron of scholars.

11: St Walter of l'Esterp (d1070); St Tudy (Tegwin, Tudinus) of Brittany (5th century).

12: St Etheihard (Aethelhard) of Canterbury; St Pancras of Rome, patron of teenagers.

13: St Merewenna of Romsey (d970); St Abban of Abingdon.

14: St John the Silent, patron of silence and floods (c482-559); St Engelmund (d739); St Matthias, patron of carpenters and tailors.

15: St Dympna, patron of nervous and mental disorders, and those suffering from incest (7th century); St Isidore the Farmer, patron of farmers and rural communities (c1110-1170); St Mary, patron of humanity; St Britwin of Beverley (d735).

16: St Carantoc (7th century), patron of Llangrannog in Wales, of Carhampton in Somerset and Crantock in Cornwall; St John Nepomucen, patron against calumnies (ca. 1330-1383); St Brendan, patron of boatmen, mariners, travellers and elderly adventurers; Octaves of the Assumption.

17: St Madern (Maden, Madron) of Cornwall (6th century). It has been suggested that he was a Christianisation of the mythical Celtic *Modron*, the mother goddess, since some aspects of the veneration at Madron's Well do appear to derive from pagan origins; St Maiduif of Malmesbury.

18: St Eric (d1151); St Merililaun of England (8th century); St Elgiva of Shaftesbury, (d944).

19: St Dunstan of Canterbury (909-988) – of noble Anglo-Saxon birth he was banished from the court for practising 'unlawful arts' and denounced as a magician; he was also a blacksmith and patron saint of armourers and gunsmiths.

20: St Ethelbert of East Anglia (d794); St Alucin of York (d804).

21: St Godric (1069-1170); St Gollen (Collen, Colan) of Llangollen, Wales (7th century); St Helena, patron of new discoveries, archaeologists, converts, difficult marriages, divorced people and empresses.

22: St Helene (Elen, Helen) of Carnarvon. Her story is told in

one of the tales associated with the *Mabinogion*. Welsh mythology remembers her as the daughter of a chieftain who lived somewhere near Caernarfon and for encouraging the building of roads across her country so that the soldiers could more easily defend it from attackers, thus earning her the name *Elen Luyddog* (Elen of the Hosts). Since many characters in these tales are thought to be Christianised reflections of older deities, it has been suggested that Elen reflects (along with Rhiannon, etc) a tradition of goddesses of sovereignty.

23: St Julia (5th century); St William of Rochester. **The *Tubilustria* of May was dedicated to Volcanus, an early Roman deity of fire and the smithy.**

24: St David of Scotland (c1085-1153); St Mary.

25: St Gregory VIII, Hildrebrand (c1021-1085); St Aldhelm (Adelemus, Athelmas, Adelnie, Eadelhelm, Aedelhem) of Malmesbury, patron of brewers (d709); Venerable Bede of Wearmouth, Jarrow; *Fors Fortuna*, a Roman festival of Fortuna, goddess of destiny.

26: St Bede (673-735); St Augustine of Canterbury (d605).

27: St Augustine, patron of theologians (d605).

28: St Germanus (c378-448); St Augustine of Canterbury (d605); Lanfranc of Canterbury (d1089).

29: St Theodosia, patron of icon painters (9th century); **Oak Apple Day commemorates the entry of Charles II into London after the Restoration in 1660;** *Ambarvalia* **was a solemn annual Roman purification of the fields, when each farmer led his household and one of his animals in a procession around the boundaries of his land.**

30: St Ferdinand III (1199-1252); St Hubert, patron of hunters (d727); St Walstan of Bawburgh (d1016) – name of a holy well revered as a sanctuary of the local pagan god of cattle and as such he became the patron saint of farms, farmers and farmhands.

31: St Winnow, Mancus and Mybrad of Cornwall (6th century).

June

01: Named for Juno, queen of the Roman gods and the guardian of women. The first half of the month was a period of religious purification and as such was an inauspicious time for marriage. The Anglo-Saxons called it 'Mow-month' or *Weyd-monath* – *'because the beats did then weyd in the meadow, that is to say, go and feed there'*. St Justin, patron of philosophers (d167); St Wistan (d850); St Ronan of Cornwall; St Candida.

02: Erasmus, patron saint of sailors (d300).

03: St Clotildis, patron of adopted children and widows (d545).

04: St Optatus (4th century); St Petroc of Padstow (6th century); St Buriana of Buryan; St Breaca (Breque, Branca, Branka), of Cornwall (5th century); St Walter of England (d1150).

05: St Boniface of Crediton (c690-775).

06: St Norbert, patron of peacemakers (1080-1134).

07: St Wulstan of Worcester; St Robert of Chichester; St Robert of Newminster, Northumberland (1100-1159); St Willibald of Wessex (d786).

08: St William, patron of orphans (d1154); St Elphege; **St Levan (Selevan) of Cornwall, possibly an assassinated Breton king (murdered kings often being sanctified after their death) and keeper of a holy well (6th century);** St Edgar Peaceful of England (d975).

09: St Columba of Iona, patron of floods, bookbinders and poets (521-597) – his feast day is said to be the luckiest day of the year in the Scottish Highlands; St Ephraem of Syria (d373); St Edmund of Canterbury; *Vestalia* honours Vesta, goddess of **hearth and home, who was worshipped in every household, while the sacred Fire of State was kept ever burning (except on 1st March, the start of the new year when it was ceremonially renewed.**

10: St Getulius (d121).

11: St Barnabas the Apostle (1ˢᵗ Century); *Matralia* **was the annual matron's festival at Rome.**

12: St Basilidis.

13: St Antony of Padua (1195-1231).

14: St Elgar of Bardsey, Wales (d1100); St Dogmail, patron saint of toddlers.

15: St Vitus, patron of dancers and actors (4ᵗʰ century); St Eadburga of Winchester (d960).

16: St Cyr of Quiricus and St Julitta (d304).

17: St Botulf, patron of travellers and some aspects of farming (d680); St Nectan (Nighton, Nectaran) of Hartland, Devon, and known for his healing well; St Briavel of the Forest of Dean; St Adulf of England (d680); St Joseph of Arimathea, patron of funerals (1ˢᵗ century).

18: St Mark (Marci) and St Marcellian (d286).

19: St Juliana Falconieri patron of sickness (1270-1340); St Romuald of Ravenna (c950-1027), Feast of the Holy Martyrs Gervase and Prothasius.

20: St Alban (d304), patron saint of the British Isles; St Edward the Martyr was killed under strange circumstances during a hunt in 978, aged 16.

21: St Maine of Saint-Meon, Brittany; **Summer Solstice;** *Solstitium* **when Sirius the 'dog star' rose from behind the sun.**

22: St Paulinus of Nola, patron of the arts (d431); St Alban, patron of converts and torture victims.

23: St Aetheldreda (Audry, Etheidreda, Ethelreda) of Ely, patron of neck and throat ailments, and widows (d678); St Bartholomew of Farne, Northumbria was a noted miracle worker (d1193).

24: Feast of the Nativity of St John. **St John's Day is considered in ancient folklore one of the great 'charmed' festivals of the year. Hidden treasures are said to lie open in lonely places,**

waiting for the lucky finder. **Divining rods should be cut on this day. Herbs are given unusual powers of healing, which they retain if they are plucked during the night of the feast;** St Germoc of Ireland (6th century); **Midsummer's Day.**

25: St William of Vercelli (1085-1142).

26: St Anthelm (1107-1178). **Death of the Emperor Julian, the first pagan martyr (d363).**

27: St Cyril of Alexandra (d444).

28: St Irenaeus of Lyons (d202); St Austell of St Neumann (6th century).

29: St Martha, patron of servants and cooks (1st century); St Peter, patron of fishermen (d64).

30: St Paul, patron of missionaries, evangelists, writers, journalists, authors, public workers, rope, saddle and tent makers (1st century); St Airick of England (12th century).

July

01: **Originally this month was called** *Quintilius* **by the Romans, but was changed to** *Julius* **in honour of Julius Ceasar. For the Anglo-Saxons it was** *Maedmonath* **from the** *meads* **or meadows being in bloom.** St Shenute (c450); St Veep (Veepu, Wennapa) of Cornwall (6th century); St Juthwara of England (7th century).

02: St Otto (d1139); St Gregory of Nazianzen (329-389); The Visitation; **St Swithun of Winchester; St Cewydd is the Welsh 'rain saint', like Medard in France, Gildas in Brittany and St Swithun in England he was associated with a pre-Christian rain day in July, when, if it rained on that day, it was believed rain would continue for 40 days. The feast day was originally 2nd July (moved to 15th after the calendar change).**

03: St Thomas. (*The Martyrology of St Jerome* mentioned the feast of Thomas the Apostle on 3rd July, the date to which the Roman celebration was transferred in 1969 from 21st

December, so that it would no longer interfere with the major ferial days of Advent.)

04: St Elizabeth of Portugal (1271-1336); Odo of Canterbury, patron of antique dealers (d959).

05: St Fragan and Gwen of England (5th century).

06: St Godelieve, patron of throat ailments and difficult marriages (d1070); St Sexburga (679-700); St Merryn of Andresey.

07: St Ethelberga (d665); St Palladius of Ireland (d450); St Willibald (d786); St Haedda of Winchester; St Thomas of Canterbury; *Nones Caprotinae* **was generally known as a Roman picnic day, when celebrations dedicated to the goddess Juno Caprotina were held al fresco in parks or outside the city in the fields. Tents and temporary shelters made from branches would be set up so that the revels could continue all night and into the following day.**

08: St Edgar (943-975); **St Withburga of East Anglia, known for Withburga's Well near her grave at Dereham (d743);** St Grimbald of New Minster, Winchester (d901).

09: St Everlid (Averil) of Wessex (7th century).

10: St Secunda and Rufina (3rd and 4th centuries); St Thurketyl (10th century).

11: St Benedict of Nursia, patron of students and cavers (c480-543).

12: St John Gaulbert, foresters, park rangers, and parks (999-1073); St Veronica, patron of laundry workers (1st century); Feast of the Translation of St Thomas the Martyr.

13: St Henry the Pious, patron of the childless and the handi-capped (972-1024).

14: St Deusdedit (d664); *Mercanus* **began six days of markets and fairs when Rome would have been full of colour.**

15: St Bonaventure, patron of bowel disorders (1221-1274); St Vladimir, patron of murders and parents with large families (995-1015): **St Swithin (Swithun) of Winchester (after the calendar change). If it rains on St Swithin's Day, it will**

continue for 40 days; St Plechelm of Northumbria (d775); St Edith of Polesworth (10th century).

16: St Osmond of Salisbury, patron of sufferers of toothache, rupture, paralysis and madness (c1099).

17: St Alexis, patron of beggars and pilgrims (d417); St Kenelm of Mercoa (d821).

18: St Elizabeth of Schonau (d1164); St Pambo of Nitria (315-385); St Edburga of Bicester (7th century).

19: St Arsenius (d449); St Gregory of Nyssa (d394); St Macrina the Younger (327-379); St Margaret the Virgin and Martyr, patron of pregnant women.

20: St Vulmar (d700); St Etheidwitha (Ealsitha) of Winchester; St Margaret of Antioch, patron of childbirth, pregnant women, dying people, kidney disease, peasants, exiles, (4th century); St Wilgefortis, patron of tribulations (11th century).

21: St Lawrence of Brindisi.

22: St Mary Magdalene, patron of apothecaries, glove makers, hairdressers, penitent sinners, perfumeries, sexual temptation and women (1st century); St Agnes, patron of virgins (d305).

23: St Birgit (Bridget) of Sweden, patron of widows (1302-1373).

24: St Christina the Astonishing, patron of insanity (1150-1224); St Lupus (427-479); St Lewina of England (5th century); St Menefrida of Tredresick, Cornwall (5th century); St Wulfhade and Ruffinus of Mercia (7th century).

25: St Christopher (3rd century), patron of bachelors, transportation, travelling, storms, epilepsy, gardeners, holy death, and toothache, but not adopted by the Church as a saint until the late Middle Ages; St James Bar Zebedee the Great (d 41); *Furrinalia* **was a Roman celebration of feasting and drinking in honour of an early-Italian earth-goddess.**

26: St Anne, patron saint of grandparents, women in labour and minors; also of sailors and a protector from storms; St Joachim is the patron of fathers, grandfathers, grandparents, married couples, cabinet makers and linen traders.

27: St Pantaleon, patron of physicians (d303).

28: St Samson (d565).

29: St Martha, patron of active, practical women (1st century); St Olaf (995-1030); St Mary (1st century); St Lazarus, patron of the poor and sick (1st century).

30: St Abdon and Sennen (d450); St Ermengytha of Minster, Isle of Thanet (d680); St Athelm of Canterbury (d923).

31: St Germanus Bishop of Auxerre (d446), St Neot of Glastonbury, patron of fish (d877).

August

01: After a revision of the Julian calendar by the Emperor, the Senate decided to honour him by renaming the month of Sextilis (sacred to Ceres) as Augustus; St Ethelwold of Winchester (c912-984); **the harvest season used to begin on 1st August and was called Lammas, meaning 'Loaf Mass' when farmers made loaves of bread from the new wheat crop and gave them to their local church; the Anglo-Saxons referred to it as the 'Harvest-month' or** *Weodmonath* **(month of weeds).** Feast of St Peter. **Lughnasadh, the Celtic feast day of the god Lugh.**

02: St Eusebius (d371); St Stephen; patron of horses (d257); St Alban, patron of refugees; St Plegimund of Canterbury (d914); St Alfreda (Afreda, Alfritha, Aelfnryth, Ethelreda) of Mercia (d795); **Death of King William Rufus in the New Forest (d1100).**

03: St Walthof of Melrose (d1160); St Lydia Purpuria.

04: St John Vianney, patron of priests – universally known as the 'Curé of Ars'.

05: St Oswald (604-642), patron of soldiers.

06: St Sixtus (d258); the Transfiguration of the Lord.

07: St Dominic, patron of astronomers (1170-1221); St Ellidius (Illog) of Himant (7th century). **The feast day of Cromn Dubh, the pre-Celtic god of the harvest and the Underworld.**

08: St Romanus Ostiarius (d258).

09: St Julian (d730).

10: St Laurence of Rome (d258), patron saint of librarians, archivists, cooks, and tanners.

11: St Susanna (d295).

12: St Clare, patron of clairvoyance, eye disease, goldsmiths, laundry, embroiders, gilders, good weather, (1193-1253); St Thomas (Thomas Hales) of Dover (d1295); St Merewenna (Merwenna, Merwinna) of Marharm, Cornwall; St James of Canterbury (d792); St Just of Cornwall.

13: St Hippolytus, patron of horses and prison guards (d252); St Radegund (518-587); St Ust (Justus) of St Just.

14: St Werenfrid of England, patron of vegetable gardens and is invoked for gout and stiff joints (d760).

15: Our Lady St Mary the Blessed.

16: St Stephen of Hungary (977-1038); St Armagillus of Wales (d570).

17: St Hyacinth, invoked by those in danger of drowning (1185-1257); St Clare of Montefalco (d1308); St James the Deacon of Northumbria (d769); St Drithelm of Melrose (d700).

18: St Helena, patron of difficult marriages (d330); St Hugh the Little of Lincoln, patron of philosophers and preachers (d1255).

19: St Canutus (d1086); St Credn of Evesham (d780).

20: St Bernard of Clairvaux, patron of candlemakers (1091-1153); St Edbert of York (d960).

22: St Symphorianus (d200); St Ethelgitha of Northumbria; St Arnulf of Eynesbury (9th century).

23: St Ebba of Coldingham (d870); *Vertumnalia* **celebrated in honour of the Roman god of orchards and fruit, Vortumnus, who presided over the changing seasons of the year. Great bonfires were lit at night in his honour and excessive merry-making took place.**

24: St Bartholomew, patron of bookbinders, butchers and

cobblers (1st century); St Ouen (c600-684).

25: St Ebbe (Ebba) (d683): St Louis, patron of tertiaries – lay men and women who do not take religious vows, but participate in the good works (1215-1270).

26: St Zephryinus (d217); St Pantagathus (Pandonio, Pandwyna), patron of physicians, midwives, livestock, and invoked against headaches, consumption, locusts, witchcraft, accidents and loneliness (10th century); St Bregwin of Canterbury (d764); St Ninian's Day.

27: St Caesarius (470-542); St Monica, patron of patience, wives, mothers, and victims of abuse (332-387); St Decuman (Dagan) of Somerset (d706).

28: St Augustine of Hippo, patron of brewers (354-430); St Rumwald of Nortumbria (d650); Feast of the Assumption. **The Church calendar was overladen with 'Marian days' – feast days for the Virgin Mary, which replaced the pagan celebrations.**

29: St Fergus (8th century); St Edwold of Cerne, Dorset (9th century).

30: St Cuthburga (d725); St Rumon (Ruan, Ronan, Ruadan) of Ireland.

31: St Aidan of Lindisfarne (d651) patron saint of fire fighters.

September

01: Seventh month of the Roman year, and sacred to Vulcan, god of fire and the blacksmith's craft. The Anglo-Saxons called it *Gerstmonath* or Barley-month with reference to the harvest of that crop, the main ingredient of the favourite alcoholic beverage. St Drithelm (d700); St Giles of Provence, patron of beggars and the disabled (7th century).

02: St William of Roskilde (d1070).

03: The start of the eleven days affected by the change to the Gregorian Calendar. St Gregory the Great of Rome, the patron saint of teachers (c540-604); St Hereswitha of

Northumbria (d690).

04: St Rose of Viterbo, miracle worker and patron of exiles, tertiaries and those rejected by religious orders (d1252); St Cuthbert of Lindisfarne, whose feast day moved to 20th March with the change of calendar; St Birinus of Dorchester, whose feast day was moved to 3rd December (d650). **The Abbots Bromley Horn Dance is an English folk dance dating back to the Middle Ages, which takes place on Wakes Monday, the day following Wakes Sunday, which is the first Sunday after 4th September. Thus it is the Monday between 6th and 12th September.**

05: St Quintin, patron of coughs and sneezes.

06: St Bega (7th century); St Augustine; St Felix, patron of spiders; Augebert of England (7th century).

07: St Cloud, patron of nail makers and invoked as a cure against carbuncles (c522-560); St Sozon rescues from suffering and disasters (4th century); St Alcmund of Hexham (d781); St Tilbert of Hexham (d789).

08: St Adrian, patron of soldiers and butchers; the birth of Virgin Mary; Feast of Angevin.

09: St Gorgonius.

10: St Nicholas of Tolentino, patron of souls in Purgatory (c1245-1306); St Justus of Canterbury (d627); St Frithestan of Winchester (d933).

11: St Protus and Hyacinth.

12: St Guy of Anderlect, patron of animals with horns, bachelors, people with epilepsy (d1012); St Eanswida of Folkestone (d640).

13: St John Chrysostom of Constantinople (d407).

14: St Notburga, patron of poor peasants and servants (d1313); Holy Cross Day, Holy Rood Day (also 3rd May).

15: St Adam of Caithness (13th century); St Merinus.

16: St Cornelius, patron of farm animals (d253); St Ninian, known for his healing abilities (d432)**; St Cyprian, patron of sorcerers**

(200-258); St Edith of Winchester; St Edith of Wilton.

17: St Hildegarde of Bingen was one of the first great German mystics, a poetess, and prophetess (1098-1179); St Lambert (d709).

18: St Hygbald (Higbald, Hugbald, Hybald) of Lincolnshire; **in Rome and Greece the Festival of the Eleusinian Mysteries was celebrated over two days.**

19: St Theodore of Canterbury (d690).

20: St Eustace, patron of hunters and fire fighters (2nd century); *Mercantus,* **a Roman four-day celebration of markets and fairs.**

21: St Matthew, patron of financiers and accountants (1st century); St Hieu of Tadcaster; **Autumn Equinox. Feast day of the pre-Celtic god of regeneration, Bran Fendigaid, or Bran the Blessed.**

22: St Maurice (d226).

23: St Adamnan, protector of women and children from the evils inseparable from war, forbidding them to be killed or made captive in times of strife (c624-704); St Thecla (Thekla) (1st century); St Cissa of Northumbria (7th century).

24: St Gerard, patron of mothers (d1046).

25: St Albert of Jerusalem (d1214); St Cosmas and Damian, patrons of pharmacists (c303); St Caian of Tregaian (5th century).

26: St Cyprian, a necromancer who travelled around the Mediterranean in order to expand his occult knowledge. It is said that Cyprian of Antioch was born in Carthage as a pagan child dedicated to the service of Apollo, Greek God of light, youth, healing, and prophecy. He entered the mysteries of Mithras at the age of seven, carried the torch of Demeter, wore the white garments of Kore, and served the serpent of Pallas.

27: St Sigebert (d635).

28: St Lioba (d782); St Wenceslas (d938); St Tetta of Wimborne (d772).

29: The Mass of the Archangels Gabriel and Michael, Michaelmas also the Feast of Saints Michael, Gabriel, Uriel and Raphael, the Feast of the Archangels, or the Feast of Saint Michael and All Angels, is an important day in the western Christian liturgical year. **In medieval England, Michaelmas marked the ending and beginning of the husbandman's year.**

30: St Jerome, patron of translators, librarians and encyclopaedists (d420); St Honorius of Canterbury, patron of bakers (d635).

October

01: **The eight month of the Roman year and sacred to Mars. The Anglo-Saxons called it** *wynmonath* **– the time of treading the wine-vats. Or** *Winterfyllith***, referring to a calendar in which the full moon of this month marked the beginning of winter;** St Bavo (d633); St Melorius (Mylor, Melar, Melorus) of Cornwall; St Remigius of Rheims, patron of those who want to make good meditations (d533).

02: St Leger (616-679).

03: St Thomas Cantelupe of Hereford (1218-1282); **Nottingham Goose Fair.**

04: St Francis the confessor of Assisi, patron of animals and nature (1181-1226); St Edwin.

05: St Maurus, patron of charcoal burners and coppersmiths (d584).

06: St Bruno, patron of those possessed (c1030-1101); St Faith, patron saint of pilgrims (3rd century); St Ceollach of Mercia (7th century).

07: **St Ositha (Osyth, Sytha) of Mercia, known for her holy spring and for the witch trials that took place in the village that commemorates her name (d700).**

08: **St Keyne (Keyna or Cain) of Wales, known for her holy well that granted dominance to one partner or the other in**

marriage (5th century); St Ywi of Lindisfarne (d690).

09: St Dionysius of Paris (Denys) (d272); St Robert Grosseteste of Lincoln (d1253); **Tewkesbury Mop Fair is the largest street fair in Gloucestershire and one of the oldest fairs in the country, that takes place annually on October 9th and 10th. Earliest records so far date the origins of the fair to the 12th century.**

10: St Gereon, invoked against headaches and migraine (d304); St Paulinus of York (584-644).

11: St Ethelburga of Barking (d675); St James (7th century); **Old Michaelmas Day falls on 11th October. According to an old legend, blackberries should not be picked after this date. This is because, so folklore goes, Satan was banished from Heaven on this day, fell into a blackberry bush and cursed the brambles as he fell into them. Farm workers, labourers, servants and some craftsmen would work for their employer from October to October. At the end of the employment (the day after Michaelmas) they would attend the Mop Fair dressed in their Sunday best clothes and carrying an item signifying their trade. A servant with no particular skills would carry a mop head – hence the phrase Mop Fair.**

12: St Edwin of Northumbria (584-633); St Wilfrid of Ripon (d709).

13: St Edward the Confessor (1002-1066) was among the last Anglo-Saxon kings of England, and usually considered the last king of the House of Wessex. *Fontinalia*, a Roman festival in honour of Fontus, the god of springs, fountains and wells.

14: St Calixtus (Callistus) (d222); St Kentigern (c516-601); St Manakus (Manaccus) of Holyhead.

15: St Wulfram of Sens (d703).

16: St Hedwiges, patron of orphans (d1243); St Gall, patron of birds (d630); St Louthiem (Luchtighem) of St Ludgran, Cornwall.

17: St Ignatius of Antioch (d107); St Etheldreda (a festival called Saint Audrey's Fair, was held at Ely on her feast day); St Ethelbert and Etheired of Eastery, Kent (d670).

18: St Luke, patron of arts and artists (1st century); St Gwen (Blanche, Wenn, Candida) of Talgrarth (5th century); St Kevoca (Keyne, Keyna, Ceinwen) of Wales (5th century).

19: St Frideswide of Oxford (680-735); St Oswald of Dorchester (d1016); St Eadnot of Dorchester (d1016); St Just (d616).

20: St Acca of St Andrew's Hexam (d740).

21: St Hilarion, patron against snake bites (c291-371); St Ursula and her *'undecim milia virgines'*, patron of students (4th century); St Tuda of Lindisfarne (d664).

22: St Donatus, protector against lightning (d876).

23: St Severinus Boethius (c480-524); St Clether of Wales (d520); St Elfeda of Glastonbury (d936); St Romanus, Bishop of Rouen (d640).

24: St Senoch (6th century); St Cadfarch of Wales (6th century); St Maelor (6th century).

25: St Crispin and St Cispinian of Rome, patrons of shoemakers (d287); St Remigius.

26: St Cedd of Lastingham, patron saint of interpreters (d664); St Cuthbert of Canterbury (d758); St Alfred the Great, patron of learning (d899); St Eadfrid of Leominster (d675).

27: St Frumentius (4th century).

28: St Eadsin of Canterbury (d1050); St Simon the Zealot, patron of woodcutters and tanners (1st century); St Jude (1st century) patron saint of lost causes, difficult cases, of things almost despaired of. **St Simon's and St Jude's Day traditionally marks the end of fine weather in the agricultural calendar.**

29: St Narcissus, patron of penitent women (2nd century); St Elfeda of Ramsey.

30: St Marcellus, patron saint of conscientious objectors to military service (d298); St Arilda of Gloucestershire; St Ethelnoth of Canterbury (11th century).

31: St Quentin or Quintinus, invoked against cough and sneezes (d287); St Wolfgang (c930-994); St Erth of Cornwall (6th century); **Samhain or Hallowe'en. John Stow in his** *Survey of London* **(1603), gives a description of the appointment of the Lord of Misrule:** *'These Lordes beginning their rule on Alhollon Eue [Halloween], continued the same till the morrow after the Feast of the Purification, commonlie called Candlemas day: In all which space there were fine and subtle disguisinges, Maskes and Mummeries, with playing at Cardes for Counters, Nayles and pointes in euery house, more for pastimes then for gaine.'*

November

01: The ninth month of the Roman year, sacred to Diana and the traditional beginning of winter; it was considered a lucky month and almost free of religious obligation. The Anglo-Saxons referred to it as *Windmonath* **(wind month) or** *Blotmonath* **(blood month) as this was the time to butcher livestock to lay down as salted meat for the winter.** All Saints' Day.

02: St Victorinus (d303); All Soul's Day; **Feast of the Ancestors.**

03: St Malachy (d1148); **St Winefride (7th century). A healing well bearing her name can be found at Holywell in Flintshire and its waters were said to help women conceive.** *Hilaria*, **a Roman harvest festival.**

04: St Vitalis (3rd century); St Birrstan (Birnstan, Brynstan) of Winchester (d934); St Clarus of Rochester.

05: St Bertrille (d692).

06: St Leonard's intercession was evoked for the release of prisoners, women in labour and the diseases of cattle (6th century); St Pinnock of Cornwall; St Leonard of Reresby (13th century).

07: St Willibrord of York (c658-739); St Cumgar of Devon.

08: St Cybi (Cuby, Kabius) of Cornwall, patron of the Brythonic

people; St Willehad of Northumbria (d789); the Synaxis of the Archangels. Archangel Gabriel has been called the leader of the heavenly hosts and brings salvation to mankind; Archangel Michael is most often invoked for protection from invasion by enemies, from civil war, and for the defeat of adversaries on the field of battle; Archangel Raphael cares for the convalescence of the ill, serves as the unseen guide for those who are travelling diligently with important chores and furthermore he is the protector of weddings and conjugal love; Archangel Uriel is a protector of mankind with deep ties to the Earth and a guide of the deceased.

09: St Theodore the Recruit (d306).

10: St Leo the Great of Rome (d461); St Justus of Rochester.

11: St Martin of Tours, patron of horses (c316-397): **Martinmas. When autumn wheat seeding was completed, and the annual slaughter of fattened cattle produced 'Martinmas beef'. Hiring fairs were held where farm labourers would seek new posts.**

12: St Ymar of Reculver (d830); St Lebuin of Ripon (d773).

13: St Abbos of Fleury (d1004); St Brice, patron or stomach ailments (d444); St Homobonus, patron of tailors and cloth workers (d1197); St Columba of Cornwall; *Feronia*, **a Roman terrestrial goddess of fertility and 'plenty of abundance'.**

14: St Lawrence of Ireland, patron of tanners, chefs and archivists (1128-1180).

15: St Albert the Great, patron of philosophers and scientists (1206-1280).

16: St Gertrude, patron of cats (d1302); St Margaret of Scotland, patron of death of children, large families and learning (d1093); St Alfrick of Canterbury (d1105).

17: St Gregory of Tours (539-594); St Hilda of Whitby (614-680); St Hugh of Lincoln, patron of sick children and adults, shoemakers and swans (1140-1200).

18: St Odo of Cluny, patron of rain (879-942); St Keverne of

Cornwall (6th century).

19: St Elizabeth of Hungary (1207-1231); St Ermenberga of Minster (d700).

20: St Edmund the Martyr of Suffolk, England (d869); **St Edmund was the patron saint of England until Edward III replaced him by associating Saint George with the Order of the Garter. The King believed England should have a fearless champion as its patron saint and not one defeated in battle;** St Eval (Uval, Urfol) of Cornwall (6th century); St Edmund Rich of Abingdon (d1242).

21: St Columbanus, patron of unity (c543-615).

22: St Cecily (Cecilia) of Rome, patron of music (d230).

23: St Clement of Rome, patron of mariners (d100).

24: St Crissogoni (Grisogori).

25: St Catherine of Alexandra (4th century), Cattern Day – a festival for young people, and for the workers in the several trades of which St Catherine was a patron; St Alnoth of Weedon (d700). **The Roman Festival of *Proserpina*, daughter of Ceres and the root meaning behind the Eleusinian Mysteries, and the beginning of winter.**

26: St Faustus (d311).

27: St James Intercisus, (d421); St Virgil (d784); **St Fergus of Ireland, known for his holy well (d721).**

28: St Valerian.

29: St Saturninus (d257); St Egelwine of Athelney (7th century).

30: St Andrew (1st century); **St Andrew's Day (Scotland).**

December

01: The tenth month of the old Roman year and sacred to Vesta; The Anglo-Saxons called it *Wintermonath*. St Eligius, patron of goldsmiths, metalworkers, coin collectors and of veterinarians (c588-659).

02: St Viviana (4th century).

03: St Lucius (d200).

04: St Barbara, patron of artillery and mining (4th century); St Osmund of Salisbury (d1099); St John of Damascus evoked against death by artillery, against explosions and fire (d749).

05: St Crispina of Tagora (d304); St Sabus (439-532). *Faunalia* **was a festival celebrated in rural areas, honouring nature and animals sacred to the Roman Faunus, god of fields and shepherds and of prophesy.**

06: St Nicholas of Myra, patron of children, sailors, captives, bankers and pawnbrokers (d342).

07: St Ambrose patron of beekeepers and learning (c340-397).

08: St Budo (6th century); The Conception of the Blessed Virgin Mary.

09: St Leocadia (d304); St Ethelgiva of Shaftesbury; *Optalia,* **celebrated Ops the Roman goddess of the harvest.**

10: St Eulalia of Merida (d304).

11: St Damascus, patron of pharmacists, icon painting and theology students (306-384); St Daniel the Stylite (408-493).

12: St Finnian (d549); St Walaric (d620); St Edburga of Kent (d751); St Agatha of England (d790), St Corentin (Cury) of Cornouaille, Quimper, Brittany.

13: St Lucy of Syracuse, patron of the blind (d304); **the Feast of St Lucy is celebrated as a festival of light and fire; a time for divination leading up to the Midwinter festivities.** St Edburga of Lyminge (7th century).

14: St Spiridon of Corfu (4th century); St Fingar of Hoyle (5th century).

15: St Maximus (d520); St Drostan.

16: St Adelaide, patron of those suffering paralysis (931-999).

17: St Olympias (c368-410); **Start of** *Saturnalia* **until 23rd December – the Festival of Saturn celebrated in Rome at the end of the vintage and harvesting with feasting and unrestrained merry-making. Feasts were provided by the temples and were open to the public; gifts were exchanged by visitors and guests.**

18: St Samthann, patron of convulsive children (d739); St Winebald of Wessex, patron of engaged couples and construction workers (d761); St Mawes of Falmouth (6th century).

19: St Nemesion (d250).

20: St Dominic of Silos, patron against rabies, rabid dogs and insects; of captives, pregnant women, prisoners and shepherds (d1073).

21: St Digain of Cornwall (5th century); St Thomas the Apostle, patron of architects; **Midwinter Festival and Winter Solstice.**

22: St Ischyrion (d250).

23: St John of Kanti (1390-1473); St Clement's Day. **Patron saint of blacksmiths and the date of the Clem Supper of horsemen.** *Laurentalia,* **festival of Acca Larentia, an early Italian goddess of the earth to whom the seed was entrusted.**

24: Mother's Night, *(Modraniht* **– Anglo-Saxon) and start of the 'Time between the Years' – the 13 Sacred Days and 12 Sacred Nights.**

25: St Anastasia, patron of widows (d304); St Alburga of Wilton (d800); Christmas Day; **Feast of Mithras, the Unconquered Sun and principal god of the Roman Legions.**

26: St Stephen, patron of horses (1st century); St Tathal of St Athan's, Gwent (6th century).

27: St John (1st century), patron saint of booksellers, art dealers and printers.

28: Holy Innocent's Day. Childermas. **Supposed to be the unluckiest day of the year.**

29: St Thomas Becket of Canterbury – little metal phials containing 'Canterbury water' – water to which drops of St Thomas's blood had been added were in huge demand across Europe.

30: St Egwin of Worcester (d717).

31: St Sylvester, patron of animals, good harvest, stone weapons (d335); **Watch Night. New Year's Eve.**

What the native people of Britain thought of this new focus of worship beggars belief. Many of the saints listed in the original medieval calendar were duplications, often associated with place names within the Catholic world and localised churchmen (and women) that had no real meaning for an unworldly people who had never heard of them before. To complicate matters further some were saints but not patrons; others were the old gods or local heroes now given a Christian identity and a special 'saint's day'. Nevertheless, *The Secret People* probably utilised the names of the saints for spell casting (as our examples show) in much the same way as the African slaves took Christian saints and grafted them onto their old gods to create Santeria.

In 1969, however, the Catholic Church removed ninety-three saints from the universal calendar and revoked their feast days when Pope Paul VI revised the canon of saints and determined that some of the names had only ever been alive as legends, or that not enough was known about them to determine their status. 'The purpose was to clean up a crowded liturgical calendar,' he said. 'They decided to remove particular feast days of those saints whose origins were shrouded in more mystery than manuscripts.' Among those demoted were some of the most popular saints such as St Christopher, St Ursula, St Nicholas and St George!

Seasonal Traditions

The world of *The Secret People* would have revolved around the home and family – just as it does today – and there are ways of celebrating the 'wheel of the year' so that non-pagan family, friends and children can participate without there being any overtly Craft tones to the festivities. The suggestions for the main festivals are celebratory rather than ritual observance, but there is always a hint of the Old Ways lurking just beneath the surface.

Winter Solstice (21st December)

This is the beginning of the magical year; the re-birth of the Unconquered Sun and, some would say the most important celebration of the year. Since it coincides with Yule and Christmas it is possible to arrange a family party to suit everyone without compromising personal beliefs. Because most of the symbols – evergreens, log fires, decorations, exchanging gifts and feasting – all hark back to pre-Christian times, the non-pagan guests will be blissfully unaware they are helping to observe a pagan celebration. This is an ideal opportunity to serve a really rich dinner to a small group of close friends, especially if everyone has to go their own separate ways for a family Christmas.

Formal Rite

Before the guests arrive, or after they have gone, pour a hefty helping of good red wine or port (or something special from the stillroom) and take it outside to offer as a libation to the spirits of the season. Those taking part should take a small sip and pass it on until the last person to share in the ritual should take a sip, raise the glass in salutation and pour the remainder onto the ground.

Yule

Yule was originally an indigenous midwinter festival celebrated by the Germanic peoples. The earliest references to it are in the form of month names, where the Yule-tide period lasted somewhere around two months in length, falling along the end of the modern calendar year between what is now mid-November and early January.

Yuletide Pot Pourri

The modern feast of Yule is associated with lovely spicy smells and nothing makes a home feel warm and welcoming as the perfume of a seasonal pot pourri. Save all the skins from any citrus fruit: oranges, satsumas, lemons, grapefruit, etc. Break them up and dry them in a basket in front of the fire. Add crushed cloves, freshly grated nutmeg, broken cinnamon sticks, crushed juniper berries, and a scattering of powdered orris root sprinkled over it with a teaspoon or two of sherry. This can be added to throughout the season, including clippings from a pine tree.

Traditional fare helps to simplify the menu from a good old-fashioned dinner to a lavish buffet, recipes for rich Yuletide cakes, mincemeat and puddings can be found in old cookery books – and can be made well in advanced to allow for maturing before being eaten. The French food writer, well known for his love of good food wrote in *Larousse Gastronomique* that in Britain, Christmas Day is celebrated gastronomically with even more splendour than in France. This elaborate feasting probably harkens back to medieval times since the English have always been more pagan in this respect than their European neighbours.

Formal Rite

The Yule log was traditionally given and once it was put on the hearth on Christmas Eve it was considered unlucky to have to light it again once been started, since it ought not go out until it has burned away. Just before supper on Christmas Eve while the Yule log is burning, all other lights are put out, and coloured candles are lit from the Yule log by the youngest person present. While they are being lit, all are silent and wish. The wish must not be told, or it will not come to pass. As soon as the candles are placed around the room the silence may be broken; they must be allowed to burn themselves out, and no other lights may be lit that night. To sit around the Yule log and tell ghost stories is a great thing to do on this special night.

Sometimes the log is sprinkled with wine before it is burnt, so that it smells nice when it is lit. Different chemicals can also be sprinkled on the log like wine to make the log burn with different coloured flames!

> Potassium Nitrate = Violet
> Barium Nitrate = Apple Green
> Borax = Vivid Green
> Copper Sulphate = Blue
> Table Salt = Bright Yellow

In some parts of the country a huge ashen faggot replaced the oak log, the thick bundle of green ash-sticks firmly held together with bands of ash, hazel or bramble. Brought into the house on Christmas Eve, an important part of the ritual was watching for the breaking of the bands in the fire and their bursting one by one was a signal for cheerful toasts.

Twelfth Night (6th January)
In medieval and Tudor England, Twelfth Night marked the end of a winter festival that started on All Hallows Eve, and much of what is now celebrated as Twelfth Night was traditional Midwinter revels. In some places, particularly south-western England, Old Twelfth Night is celebrated on 17th January according to the old Julian calendar. Customs vary across the world (others also being relics of the Roman Saturnalia and the Julian calendar), including concealing a dried pea or bean inside a cake, or drawing lots with beans to see who would be King and Queen of Misrule. The finders then set the pace for the evening's revels although an ideal theme would be a fancy dress party with plenty of mulled wine or ale, and rich food. Robert Herrick's poem *Twelfe-Night, or King and Queene*, published in 1648, describes the election of king and queen by bean and pea in a plum cake, and the homage done to them by the draining of Wassail bowls of 'lamb's-wool', a drink of sugar, nutmeg, ginger and ale.

The pagan party animal will have a circle of friends that

allows them to celebrate the season from Saturnalia on the 17th December to Twelfth Night on 6th January. Most of these festivities go back to ancient times and there is a great deal of fun to be had in resurrecting them in order to celebrate the turning of the year in a way that is part of our island history – even if our immediate family doesn't realise what's going on! If there's been too much partying then have a quiet 'at home' and watch one of the many versions of Shakespeare's play *Twelfth Night, or What You Will* that was written to be performed as a Twelfth Night entertainment. The play has many elements that are reversed in the tradition of Twelfth Night, such as a woman Viola dressing as a man and a servant Malvolio imagining that he can become a nobleman.

Formal Rite

Since this marks the last of the Yuletide celebrations it would be fitting to toast the forthcoming year and your expectations with a glass of cider – and if you have fruit trees pour a symbolic libation around the roots.

Imbolc or Candlemas (2nd February)

This is another good opportunity to party as the country is still in the depths of winter, despite the fact that it coincides with the start of the old Celtic lambing season, so it's a time for a celebration of new beginnings. Although formal dinner parties have gone by the board, small supper parties are still one of the best ways of entertaining a few friends at home. Despite the work involved, this is a very pleasant way to give and repay hospitality, and one where conversation can be enjoyed with those whom you wish to invite into your home. Guests may not necessarily be of pagan persuasion, but this is a time for sharing and promises for the future – so if nothing else, it can be looked upon as a ritual gesture of friendship.

For the ancestors this would have been a time when food was

running low and so much of what you'd get if you went to visit would be 'pot luck'. The number of guests would largely depend on the size of the kitchen and emphasis should be simplicity and a candle-lit room. Keep the food simple and serve a warming casserole thickened with vegetables and served with rice or fresh bread. This represents the huge stew pot of Ceridwen that was never empty.

A Weather Prophecy

If Candlemas be fair and bright, winter will have another flight; but if Candlemas brings clouds and rain, winter is gone and won't come again.

Formal Rite

This is a time for sharing, so offer food to the wildlife around your home with a formal message of: 'Eat and be welcome'...which doesn't mean chasing off the bigger birds and squirrels. They need help at this time, too.

Vernal or Spring Equinox (21st March)

The spring festival offers the opportunity to resurrect another truly traditional custom in celebrating the festival of the Anglo-Saxon deity, Ēostre. In both name and function she is personified as the rising sun, not with the time of day (dawn) but with the season – spring and what better day to celebrate than at the Vernal or Spring Equinox. Ēostre is mentioned by Bede in his 8th century work *The Reckoning of Time*, where he states that during *Ēosturmōnat* (the equivalent of April), pagan Anglo-Saxons had held feasts in Ēostre's honour, but that this tradition had died out by his time, replaced by the Christian Paschal month, a celebration of the resurrection of Jesus.

In its turn, Easter in the medieval period was calculated against the Julian calendar as falling on the first full moon after the Vernal Equinox, March 21. The full moon that precedes Easter is called the Paschal moon, and the Sunday after the Paschal full moon may be anywhere between March 21 to April 18; therefore the possible dates for Easter are from March 22 to April 25.

Corn-showing was an old semi-magical farming custom that took place on the afternoon of Easter Sunday, when the bailiff and farm workers, together with their families and friends, went to honour the wheat-fields and feasted upon plum cake and old cider. Then they joined hands and walked over the field saying: *'Every step a reap, every reap a sheaf/And God sent the master a good harvest.'*

Formal Rite

For an appropriate meal on this traditional spring festival, consider a lamb dish of some kind to share with family and friends as a formal Sunday lunch or supper party.

Beltaine Eve or May Day (31st April)

Traditionally this is to celebrate 'bringing home the may (hawthorn)' with all its attendant sensual overtones of the festival. Ideally it is an evening that should be spent at home with your partner for a special meal of your favourite foods. It is still cool enough to warrant a fire being lit and so plan to spend the evening by fire and candle light. Wise women shouldn't need lessons on how to invite some romance in, since this is a service they would have provided for the young, local girls throughout the year!

May Day Dew

Make a point of getting up early and go out into the garden to collect the early morning dew from the grass in which to bathe your face. May dew, gathered early on May Day from underneath an oak tree, was a custom that was observed by the women of all classes – in 1667 Samuel Pepys recorded in his famous *Diary* that his wife followed the custom. The charm would keep them beautiful and ensure good luck for the coming year.

Formal Rite

On the other hand, if you live alone, this festival could present the opportunity to work a solitary ritual on one of the most important days in the modern witch's calendar. Being one of the traditional Fire Festivals, Beltaine Eve is a wonderful time to hold a bonfire in the garden. It is also worth bearing in mind that magically Beltaine is part of the natural tides and not a fixed date on a calendar – so wait until the flowering of the may (hawthorn) and make the most of Nature's energies. As Fiona Walker-Craven commented in *13 Moons*:

> It is often the case that a times like this, when the old magic is closer to the surface, that those celebrating a solitary rite can have beautiful and enlightening experiences which are deeply personal and reassuring. I would go so far as to say that these stunning revelations usually only happen when one is alone with the elements.

Whitsun Ale (23rd May)

...that at the high feast of Pentecost especially, afore al other high feasts in the yeare, he would not goe that day to meat until he had heard or seene some great adventure or mervaile. And for that custom all manner of strange adventures came before King Arthur at that feast afore all other feasts.
(Morte d'Arthur, chapter cxviii. Sir Thomas Malory)

A 'Whitsun Ale' was a parish celebration held originally to raise money for church funds, when the whole village would take a day off and as the name suggests a large quantity of ale would be brewed for the festival. The custom mirrored the courtly practice of holding feasts and tournaments at Whitsuntide as described by Thomas Malory. A Whitsun Ale was a very big affair in most villages and an edict of Queen Elizabeth I in 1569 gives some idea of what might have taken place:

> ...*the shooting with the standard, the shooting with the broad arrow, the shooting at twelve score prick, the shooting at the Turk, the leaping for men, the running for men, the wrestling, the throwing of the sledge, and the pitching of the bar, with all such other games as have at any time heretofore or now be licensed, used, or played.*

According to Church tradition, Pentecost was always about seven weeks after Easter Sunday, or 50 days after Easter, including Easter Day. In Orthodox churches, Whitsunday was observed after the date set by the western Church because some Orthodox churches still observed holidays according to the Julian calendar.

Formal Rite

People enjoy family gatherings, picnics, or outings to the country because Whitsunday was linked to pagan spring rites, such as the English custom of Morris dancing.

Summer Solstice or Litha (21st June)

The longest day of the year and a good time for a summer garden party complete with lanterns and a fire of some sort. The party can be as modest or lavish as you choose, and it can also be a time to catch up with people you haven't seen for a long time. Renew old friendships and introduce some new ones as the mingling crowd make sure that incompatible people aren't lumped together for the whole evening. This is a time for sun and lightness and any entertainment or theme should reflect this sentiment.

Formal Rite

Toast the longest day with homemade elderflower wine or a

commercially produced elderflower *pressé* before the guests arrive or after they have left. Pour your libation on the ground in the direction of the setting sun.

Lammas or Lughhnasad (1st August)

This was the traditional start of autumn when everyone would be working late in the fields in order to gather in the harvest. There would be six weeks of intense labour and in the kitchen there would be plenty going on in terms of bottled fruit, pickles and preserves for the coming winter. *The Secret People* would be utilising the natural harvest and be busy drying herbs and preparing potions for the months ahead when fresh ingredients wouldn't be available.

The Lammas Cake

8oz self-raising flour
5oz butter
1 teaspoon mixed spice
5oz caster sugar
6oz currants
6oz sultanas
2oz chopped peel
2 eggs beaten with 6 tablespoons of milk

Mix the flour and spices; beat the butter and sugar to a cream. Beat the eggs and milk together and alternately stir the flour and egg/milk mixture to the butter and sugar, a little at a time. Add the fruit and mix thoroughly. Bake for 2½ hours, first at Gas Mark 5 (350F/180C) for 1 hour then reduce to Gas Mark 2 (300F/150C).

This is also the time for thanksgiving and contemplation of the last year's work; of the harvest and the hunt; symbolised by the season of 'Lammas growth' when, according to Even John Jones in *Witchcraft – A Tradition Renewed*, the 'old sacred oaks of Britain put forth a new young growth of leaves'.

Formal Rite

It was on the 'morrow of Lammas' that William Rufus met his mysterious death beneath the oak trees and reinforced the legend of the sacrificial king. It is also a strange time since it is possible that the festival itself once coincided with the Summer Solstice – Lugh being the old Celtic sun-god. With all the alterations to the calendar and the constant precession, time certainly hasn't stood still – but whichever way we see it, Lughnasad is very much a male festival and so any celebration of this most sacred of times should reflect this.

Autumn Equinox or Mabon (21st September)

A good time for a traditional Harvest Home and the chance to prepare a real harvest supper that offers all the things that would have been found waiting at supper time in a farm house kitchen after a long day in the fields. Here the emphasis is on the past and what has been grown in the kitchen garden. The supper should be eaten outside where possible, or around the kitchen table, as this would have been a 'working meal'. Ideally it's the sort of supper where each of the guests can provide one of the courses or the appropriate drink. To set the atmosphere, display any freshly prepared produce for decoration as this will be a personal harvest celebration. Give each of the guests a small jar of pickles or jam as a gift in a gesture of sharing. The background music can be traditional folk songs or medieval tunes.

Traditional Harvest Home Supper

Nourishing home-made soup with lots of fresh, crusty bread and oodles of real butter.

For the main course, choose between a baked ham or game pie, served either hot or cold with green vegetables and jacket potatoes; or with salad and plenty of home-made pickles.

Follow this by home-made apple pie with cream and a selection of cheeses served with celery.

Formal Rite

Before the end of the meal make sure everyone's glass is full and propose a toast to the bounty of the harvest and, if performing the rite out of doors, pour an extra glass in libation on the ground in honour of John Barleycorn.

Michaelmas (11th now 29th September)

This was the time when farm folk calculated how many animals they could afford to feed over the winter and how many would have to be sold, or slaughtered and salted down in order to preserve the meat for winter. In addition to livestock fairs, rural people attended hiring fairs, which were especially important for farm labourers looking for winter employment after the harvest. Michaelmas was one of the regular quarter-days for settling rents and accounts; often, since this was also the time of the 'geese harvest', many a farmer paid off his accounts with a brace or more of plump birds from the flock hatched in the spring. During the Middle Ages, St Michael's Day was a great religious feast in most of western Europe, coinciding as it did with the end of the harvest.

Formal Rite

In England it was the custom to eat a goose on Michaelmas, which was supposed to protect against financial need for the next year. *'He who eats goose on Michaelmas day shan't money lack or debts to pay.'*

Samhain or Hallowe'en (31st October)

Although Samhain is not a time for celebration and rejoicing, a Hallowe'en party is a way of inviting non-pagans to take part in this ancient observance. Fancy dress is good, complete with cups of blood (tomato soup) and dead men's fingers (sausages) if catering for kids – or perhaps something a little more sophisticated if you insist on being grown up about it. If catering for non-pagan guests it's wiser to focus on the pleasantly superstitious side of Hallowe'en rather than on the more Otherworldly elements that would normally be observed in private.

For a party, the decorations are just as important as the food, with rooms dimly lit by candles and firelight. Plenty of evergreen foliage with black and silver ribbons can look extremely effective – and not forgetting the traditional hollowed-out turnips to hold tea-lights. Many games for this time are associated with fortune-telling as this was the old year end, and people are always anxious to know what the coming year has in store. This doesn't mean compromising personal scrying or divinational skills – as this can be extremely dangerous – but a bran tub or wheel of fortune with suitable gifts that participants can interpret for fun would be fine. But definitely no mirrors or ouija boards!

Ducking or Bobbing for Apples

This ancient game can be made even more fun if a small piece of paper is hidden inside the apples on which is written a forfeit and/or prize. The game is played by trying to catch the floating apples in the teeth...but be warned the floor will get soaked

Formal Rite

In paying homage to the Ancestors it is important to place a lighted candle in the window to invite them in, and in more formal circumstances it is well to offer a 'dumb supper' – and set aside a plate set for any Otherworldly guests.

If, as it should be, for *The Secret People*, all these observations are a way of life rather than something they do one night a week – i.e. Thursday night witches – then it may not always be possible to celebrate traditional days with ritual observance.

In fact, much of what passes for Craft today has its roots in ritual magic rather than traditional rural witchcraft. In the old days the 'wheel of the year' would have been celebrated with festivity and celebration because it would have been seen as a form of thanksgiving in a natural and pleasurable way rather than ritual observance. These were probably the only feast days that rural folk allowed themselves as a break from the daily chores of working on and with the land.

Chapter Eight

The Country Calendar

The country or farming calendar starts in October at Michaelmas, which used to fall on 11th of the month according to the old calendar – but has now moved to the 29th because by ancient custom most farms were rented from the Old Michaelmas. The seasons, however, do not comply with set dates on a printed calendar and *The Secret People* practised their arts according to Nature's timing...when certain plants and flowers were in bloom.

October

Most of the grain harvest would be in by now, but there were still some 'dirty' crops to be raised – sugar beet and other root crops that were grown for feeding livestock during the winter. The farmer will be ploughing under the stubble of the old wheat crop and the frosts that are sure to follow in late October will crumble the earth to make the arduous task of aerating the soil considerably easier. Unless the weather is unduly wet, the fields were prepared for sowing wheat to be harvested the following August.

Out in the countryside there are berries to be picked from the elder tree for making wine and, after the first frost, sloes are ready for harvesting for the annual supply of sloe gin (see Chapter Two: The Goodwife – Stillroom). Hedge bindweed will still be flowering if the weather is mild and has been considered a nuisance for centuries. According to *Country Seasons*, by Philip Clucas: *'Even in herbalism it was regarded as no fit object for a country cure, being hurtful in every respect.'*

November

The month is dark, wet and foggy and little can be done on the farm apart from hedging and ditching. Cattle would be brought into the stockyard if the land was heavy and wet, where they were fed and sheltered from bad weather. A dank landscape, steeped in mist from morning to noon, waits for winter to fulfil its yearly task.

Out in the countryside the only plant that can still be freshly picked is the humble chickweed (*stellaria media*) that grows all year round. At this time of the year sprigs can be added to salads or cooked as a vegetable. Chickweed has been used as a healing herb of centuries and Culpeper's recipe for ointment was:

> *Boil a handful of Chickweed, and a handful of red rose leaves [petals] dried, in a quart of muscadine, until the fourth part be consumed; then out to them a point of oil of trotters of sheep's feet; let them boil a good while, still stirring them well; which being strained, anoint the grieved place therewith, warm against the fire, rubbing it well with one hand.*

In modern herbalism the plant is used internally for rheumatism and externally for itching skin conditions, eczema, psoriasis, vaginitis, ulcers, boils and abscesses.

December

The fields have changed colour as the yellow stubble of the cornfields and the grey-green of old hayfields are turned over by the plough. The countryside is alive with the cries of gulls, lapwings, rooks and starlings gobbling up the grubs and worms turned up in the process. Each year the crops are rotated to keep the land healthy. Rooks circle noisily overhead, then vanish to their roosts as the winter sun sets.

Out in the countryside the only colours to be seen in the hedgerows are the scarlet berries of the **holly** and the hips of the **wild rose** (*rosa canna*). Rose hips, rich in vitamin C, were made into syrup, that could be added to cough mixtures or used to flavour medicines. The hips were also made into syrups and jam, and for making wine or vinegar. Pureed fruit, deseeded and mixed with wine and sugar, was served as a dessert in the Middle Ages.

Holly (*ilex aquifolium*) berries are poisonous, being violently emetic and purgative, but have been used to treat dropsy. Culpeper said: *'The bark and leaves are excellent, being used in fomentations for broken bones, and such members as are out of joint.'*

In addition to its own inherent medicinal properties, mistletoe (*viscum album*) was also reputed to possess those of its host plant. Although poisonous, it was prescribed for heart diseases, high blood pressure, rheumatism, gout, nervous disorders, and tumours. Culpeper said that it was so highly esteemed by some that *'they have called it Lignum Sanctae Crucis, wood of the holy cross, believing it help the falling sickness, apoplexy and palsy, very speedily, not only to be inwardly taken, but to be hung at their neck.'*

January

In warmer parts of the country the first lambs are appearing, but there are no cattle in the fields because there is no grass in the pastures. January is the cruellest of months – one of extreme cold and bitter testing, but to wander woods and meadows thick with snow is to encounter an enchanted world where the normal laws of nature seem suspended.

Out in the countryside, spring often begins in December... because it is in December that the first snowdrop pushes its tip into the low sunlight. **Snowdrops** (*galanthus nivalis*) are the flower of flowers in January and although the plant is poisonous, it was used in the Middle Ages to promote menstrual discharge and ease digestive disorders. The crushed bulbs were applied as a poultice to ease frostbite. It was mentioned by herbalist Gerard, but not by Culpeper.

Neither is **gorse** (*ulex europaeus*) any more a flower of January than in other months of the year because as one old country proverb says: *'When the gorse is out of flower kissing's out of season.'*

January sun is uncertain, shining between snow and fog, but when it shines it lights the yellow bloom of the gorse with a new radiance. Yellow is the first colour of flowers in spring and wild aconites also reflect the winter sun. Listed by Aelfric, gorse was used in a decoction made from the flowers and prescribed for jaundice and kidney complaints. A more modern, but traditional, recipe is used by Whitby fishermen to protect their hands and help heal cracks caused by cold and sea water.

Whitby Gorse Salve

Melt a lump of lard gently and add as many gorse flowers as the lard will take. Leave overnight in a warm place for the lard to absorb the goodness from the flowers. Ideally, the mixture should be just warm enough to keep the lard liquid. Next day re-melt the mixture, strain out the flowers through muslin, then add more fresh flowers and leave overnight again. Repeat this several times until the lard has taken on a good yellow colour from the flowers; then it is ready to use.

February

The fields this month are flecked with the green bloom of new wheat and although it all seems dull and cheerless, the year is beginning to turn and more lambs can be seen in the fields. It was anciently believed that the heaviest snowfall occurred on St Dorothea's Day – 6th February.

In February the fields and woods awake and the **hazel** (*corylus avellana*) shakes out her yellow veil of catkins in the hedgerow. Listed by Aelfric, the leaves, bark and flowers had various medicinal uses, including the treatment of varicose veins, circulatory disorders, menstrual problems, haemorrhoids and slow healing wounds. Culpeper said that the nuts, *'sprinkled with pepper draws rheum from the head'*.

The **lesser celandine** (*ranunculus ficara*) grows on the woodland floor, moist fields and in the ditches. Also known as pilewort, it was recommended by Culpeper to be used in a decoction of the leaves and root and made into an ointment in the treatment of haemorrhoids and the 'king's-evil'.

Coltsfoot (*tussilago farfara*) graces railway banks and stony roadsides – gold to be found on a rubbish heap – and is an ancient treatment for coughs and colds. Listed by Aelfric, Gerard and Culpeper, the herb was applied externally to soothe irritation, reduce swellings and heal skin ulcers; and used in the form of a syrup for bronchitis and asthma.

Common periwinkle (*vinca major*) that grows in wild places with its trailing stems and pale blue flowers was listed by Aelfric to check internal bleeding, heal sores, wounds and ulcers, soothe inflammations, relieve cramps, and reduce blood pressure and nervous tension. Culpeper said it *'is a great binder, and stays bleeding at the mouth and nose, if it be chewed'*. The plant can be poisonous.

Mezereum (*daphne mezereum*) with its rose-purple clusters and sweet perfume was recommended by Culpeper for use in an ointment prepared from the bark or the berries for the treatment of *'foul ill-conditioned ulcers'*. Despite the plant's poisonous nature it is still used in homoeopathic form for mental depression.

March

On the farm March can be one of the busiest months of the year, or the most frustrating if it happens to be wet. Although wheat can be sown in mud, oats and barley must be drilled into a couple of inches of dry soil. The grass in the pastures is usually showing signs of growth again. March often 'comes in like a lion' with buffeting easterly winds, rain showers and occasional flurries of snow.

In the woods and hedgerows **primroses** (*primula vulgaris*) are blooming and often used in love potions, and in charms to protect against evil. Medicinally the dried and powdered root was taken as a treatment against nervous disorders, gout and rheumatism, it was mentioned by Gerard and Culpeper.

The most magical of flowers to be found in the landscape is the white blossom of the **blackthorn** (*prunus spinosa*) that flowers on the bare, black wood of the branches. Blackthorn flowers were used as a tonic and a mild laxative; the leaves used as a mouthwash and to stimulate the appetite; the bark to reduce fever; and the fruit for bladder, kidney and digestive disorders.

The roots and stems of **butcher's broom** (*ruscus aculeatus*) was prescribed by Dioscorides and other ancient physicians for treating kidney stones; the roots and young stems were traditionally used to treat haemorrhoids, gout and jaundice. It reduced inflammation, increased perspiration and acted as a mild laxative. The young shoots were eaten like asparagus, to which the plant is related. A decoction of the dried root is still recommended in the treatment of jaundice, urinary stones and the suppression of menstruation.

Butterbur (*petasites hybridus*) is so-called because its leaves are so large and soft that they were once used to wrap butter. Culpeper wrote of it: *'The roots are used against the plague and pestilential fevers by provoking sweat. The powder taken in wine resisteth the force of any other poison.'* It is a heart tonic and a diuretic.

The common **dandelion** (*taraxacum officinale*) often known as piss-a-bed due to its diuretic properties, was recommended by Culpeper for *'removing obstructions of the liver, gall-bladder and spleen'* and is used today for urinary problems.

Dog's mercury (*mercurialis perennis*) is extremely poisonous if used fresh. Culpeper described it as *'there is not a more fatal plant than this'* and although homoeopaths make a tincture from the fresh plant for treating rheumatism and gastro-intestinal upsets, it is not used by herbalists, nor recommended for domestic use.

Towards the end of the month the clustered blossoms of the **elm** (*ulmus campestris*) put on their crimson show. The dried inner bark is a tonic, astringent and diuretic; formerly used in the treatment of certain *'cutaneous diseases of a leprous character, such as* *ringworm'*. It was applied both externally and internally. A homoeopathic tincture is made of the inner bark, and used as an astringent. A medicinal tea was also formerly made from the flowers.

One time-honoured spring rite is the gathering of the catkins of the **goat-sallow** or 'pussy willow' (*salix caprea*). Willows are important medicinal plants and the bark of all *salix* species contains salicin; a compound which can relieve pain and fever and from which aspirin was derived.

Ground ivy (*glechoma hederacea*) is that blue-flowered carpet of hedge-banks and field margins. In the 2nd century AD, Galen recommended the use of ground ivy to treat inflamed eyes and cure failing eyesight. Culpeper said: that the *'juice dropped into the ear doth wonderfully help the noise and singing of them, and helpeth the hearing which is decayed.'*

Ladysmock (*cardamine pratensis*) is commonly known as cuckoo flower. It contains Vitamin C and according to Culpeper was used to treat scurvy; it also has tonic and expectorant properties making it useful in treating coughs. It can be used fresh in salads just like watercress. *The flowers of the ladysmock and kingcup are ideal for use in a 'money' charm as they represent 'gold and silver' and this poem can be adapted to use as a chant while spell-casting. 'Ladysmocks silver, kingcups gold,/These are the meadow's wealth untold./Gleaming in sunlight, a joy to behold...'* **Marsh marigold** (*caltha palustris*) or kingcups that grow by the stream are highly poisonous and the plant juices can cause blistering or inflammation on skin or mucous membranes on contact, and gastric illness if ingested.

The brightest of all wild flowers of the stubble-field that blooms all year round, and one of the first to be noticed in March, is the **scarlet pimpernel** (*anagallis arvensis*). Once highly regarded as a medicinal herb with uses dating back to Pliny and Dioscorides, it is no longer considered safe by most herbalists except for external use as a water for improving the complexion, especially for freckles.

White (*lamium album*) and purple **dead nettle** flower for most of the summer and the white variety, also known as Archangel has been used for gynaecological and obstetric problems since at least medieval times. The **purple** variety (*lamium purpureum*) is astringent, diaphoretic, diuretic, purgative and styptic. The herb and flowers, either fresh or dried, have been used to make a decoction for checking any kind of haemorrhage; the leaves are also useful to staunch wounds, when bruised and outwardly applied. The dried herb, made into a tea and sweetened with honey, promotes perspiration and acts on the kidneys, being useful in cases of chill. The Swedish botanist, and physician, Carl Linnaeus, reported that this species also has been boiled and eaten as a pot-herb by the peasantry in Sweden.

Wild daffodils (*narcissus pseudonarcissus*) are only a foot high and grow in damp meadows and pastures and although recommended by Culpeper for a variety of complaints, modern research says it is not recommended for domestic use because of its toxic qualities.

April
Everything is getting greener day by day and the water meadows on which the cattle are grazing are lush. Roots crops would be sown for harvesting later in the year. It is a month of unfolding buds, or warmth and cold, sunshine and showers.

Among the April flowers come the **bluebells** (*hyacinthoides non-scripta*) and although abundant in medieval woodland, it is not mentioned in British herbals before the 16th century. Although poisonous when fresh, dried bulbs were powdered and used to stem bleeding and increase the production and discharge of urine.

The perennial children's favourites, **buttercups** (*ranunculaceae*) and **daisies** (*bellis perennis*) are in flower this month. The former, however, are poisonous and will cause blisters to appear on the skin if the foliage remains in contact for any length of time, that are slow to heal. Culpeper referred to it as *'this furious biting herb'*. Daisies, on the only hand were mainly used in an ointment to help heal wounds and bruises. An infusion of the flowers was used as a skin tonic. Perhaps the association of the two flowers is similar to the way stinging nettles and dock leaves grow side by side.

Delicate **cowslip** (*primula veris*) leaves were used as a salve for healing wounds and the flowers used as a mild laxative. Cowslip tea was recommended for headaches, insomnia and nervous tension. The root was prescribed for whooping cough and bronchitis. The leaves and flowers were eaten in salads and the flowers used to make cowslip wine.

Brightly dressed **lords and ladies** (*arum maculatum*) or **cuckoo pint**, common throughout spring in almost every hedgerow, acquired its name because of the likeness to male and female genitalia. In Elizabeth I's time the plant was known as starch-wort because the roots were then used for supplying pure white starch to stiffen the ruffs and frills worn at that time by gallants and ladies. Although it had numerous medicinal uses in the past, it does contain poisonous and purgative substances and is not recommended for domestic use.

Orchis (*orchis ornithophora folio maculoso*) are also known as fox-stones. Gerard said of the plant: *'There is no great use of these in physic but they are chiefly regards for the pleasure and beautiful flowers, wherein Nature hath seemed to play and disport herself.'* Culpeper, however, listed several uses including killing worms in children, healing the king's evil, not to mention that it could: *'provoke venery, strengthening the genital parts and helping conception'*.

Violets (*viola odorata*) can be found on warm, sunny banks and at the edge of the woods. According to Culpeper: *'The leaves are antiseptic and are used internally and externally for the treatment of malignancies.'*

Delicate **wood anemones** or windflowers (*anemone nemorosa*) appear in the woods. During medieval times the juice of the plant was prescribed externally for leprosy. Mixed with hog's grease it was used as an ointment for scalds and ulcers. Modern research has revealed that the herb is potentially poisonous.

May

By now nearly all the fields, hedgerows and the trees in the wood and coppice are green; all the cattle are in the fields day and night. The first silage cutting depends on good weather and the hours are long when trying to get it into the silo before the rain comes. May well deserves its folk title, 'The Month of Flowers'.

Broom (*planta genista*) was mainly prescribed for heart and circulatory disorders, but was also used for kidney and bladder complaints. Culpeper recommended it for dropsy, gout, sciatica and pains of the hips and joints. The young branches boiled in oil were used to kill head and body lice. In large doses broom is dangerous and also mildly narcotic. The plant was the badge of the Plantagenet kings.

By the stream, in woods, copses and in damp shady areas, the **blue bugle** (*ajuga reptans*) grows and Culpeper says: *'The decoction of the leaves and flowers made in wine and taken will dissolve congealed blood in those that are bruised inwardly by a fall.'* The whole herb is collected from late spring and dried. It has aromatic and astringent properties, and can be used for arresting internal haemorrhages.

Greater bindweed (*calystegia sepium*) was used in herbal medicine as a laxative and purgative. Applied externally as a poultice the fresh leaves of the plant were said to burst a boil within 24 hours.

The cuckoo's call echoes across the land and **hawthorn** (*crataegus monogyna*) in bloom transforms the landscape. Hawthorn was mainly used to treat heart and circulatory disorders. Culpeper said: *'The seeds in the berries beaten to a powder* *being drunk in wine, are good against the stone and dropsy.'*

In ancient Greece, **hemlock** (*conium maculatum*) was used for executing convicted criminals and lawbreakers and Culpeper warned that: *'Hemlock is exceedingly cold, and very dangerous, especially to be taken inwardly.'* Although highly poisonous, it was valued for its sleep-inducing, antispasmodic and pain-relieving properties. In the Middle Ages the plant was used to treat epilepsy, nervous spasms, mania, St Anthony's fire and St Vitus's Dance. Externally the leaves were used to heal sores and ulcers, and reduce inflammation. It is not recommended for domestic medicine.

Heartease (*viola tricolour*) is mildly laxative, diuretic, diaphoretic and expectorant. It is also considered to be a good blood purifier. An infusion is recommended for skin eruptions in children, catarrh and asthma. The dose is half a teaspoon of the powered leaves in a cupful of boiling water.

Herb Robert (*geranium robertianum*) is common on waste ground, woodland and banks of ditches and used as a compress for healing wounds. Culpeper says: *'It speedily heals wounds and is effectual in old ulcers in the privy parts or elsewhere. A decoction of it has been of service in obstructions of the kidneys and in gravel.'*

Lily of the valley (*convallaria majalis*) needs caution when handling as an overdose can cause severe vomiting and purging. Culpeper said that: *'The spirit of the flowers distilled in wine helped palsy, is good in apoplexy and comforts the heart.'* Although potentially poisonous, lily of the valley was used to treat gout, sore eyes, poor memory, loss of speech and heart disease. The dried and powdered root was used as snuff to clear nasal mucous and relieve headaches.

Rosebay willowherb (*chamerion angustifolium)* also known as fireweed, reflects the plant's appearance following forest fires and other events which leave the earth scorched. This tendency to appear from scorched earth also gave rise to the name 'bombweed' during the Second World War, when the plant quickly populated derelict bomb sites. A decoction is made from the dried herb and powdered root for digestive disorders accompanied by diarrhoea. It is soothing and astringent. The dried leaves can be made as a tea.

Saxifrage or **great burnet** (*pimpinella saxifraga*) grows at the edge of the wood and in hedgebanks. The root is good for the colic and expels wind. *'The juice of the herb dropped into bad wounds in the head, dries up their moisture and heals them.'* Burnet saxifrage, or lesser burnet is more popular with herbalists. Held in high esteem by the ancients, saxifrage was also added to salads, cakes, sauces, soups, fish and vegetable dishes, and used to flavour alcoholic drinks. A native of Britain, burnet saxifrage is a member of the *umbelliferae* (parsley) family, and is neither a burnet nor a saxifrage.

Watercress (*rorippa nasturtium-aquatica*) is to be found in shallow flowing water by a sunny bank. Traditionally taken as a spring tonic, the leaves are added to salads, to garnish butter, made into soup and a sauce for fish. Internally it has been taken for oedema, catarrh, bronchitis, anaemia, debility associated with chronic disease and gall bladder complaints.

The fruit, bark and gum of **wild cherry** (*prunus avium*) trees were used to soothe irritating coughs, treat bronchial complaints and improve digestion. Although the wild cherry, listed by Aelfric, is a native to Britain, it is thought the Romans introduced the cultivated variety. Culpeper also recommended its use for a variety of complaints.

Wild strawberry (*fragaria vesca*) is found in woods and shady places, hedgerows and roadsides. The berries were used for a wide variety of cures and Gerard said: *'The distilled water drunk with white wine is good against the passion of the heart, reviving the spirits and making the heart merry.'* The fruit was used in cosmetics and the dried leaves were added to pot-pourri.

Woodruff (*gallium odoratum*) grows in woods and on shady banks and was used as a strewing herb in the Middle Ages.

Garard said: '*Being made up into garlands or bunches, and hanged up in houses in the heat of summer, doth very well attempter the air, cool and make fresh the place, to the delight and comfort of such that are therein.*' As a medicinal herb Culpeper said: '*It opens obstructions of the liver and spleen and is said to be a provocative to venery. It is good for weak consumptive people*'.

Wood sorrel (*oxalis acetosella*) can be found in moist and shady spots in woodland or beside hedges. The plant is particularly rich in oxalic acid and potassium oxalate, which is not suitable for those with gouty or rheumatic tendencies. It can be injurious if prescribed injudiciously and excessive or prolonged administration is not recommended.

June

Although June is the hay-making month with the longest days of the year, it often has very patchy weather. Everyone remembers it being sunny all day long, with just a gentle breeze to ripple the ripe hay now about two feet high – but it wasn't always like that. The decision to cut is when the grass is in flower, but not in seed, while the clovers, shorter than the rippling grass, will be showing pink and crimson flowers underneath. Towering oaks cast heavy shadows over leaf-bound lanes, while in the distance hills are obscured by a shimmering heat-haze.

Columbine (*aquilegia vulgaris*) is a cultivated plant, but is occasionally found in the wild growing in woodland clearings. Culpeper said: '*The seed taken in wine causeth a speedy delivery of women in childbirth.*' Modern herbalists, however, do not use the plant as it is slightly poisonous, but it has astringent properties and can be used externally as a lotion.

Common bryony (*bryonia dioica*) is another poisonous plant that has been valued medicinally since ancient times. Listed by Aelfric it grew wild in British hedgerows and was cultivated in physic gardens. Taken internally in small doses it was used in the treatment of rheumatism, sciatica and chest complaints;

externally it was used to treat leprosy, old sores, gangrene and other skin ailments. In medieval times the juice, mixed with deadly nightshade (*atropa belladonna*), was used as an anaesthetic. Culpeper said it was not to be rashly taken.

Clover, white (*trifolium repens*) and red (*trifolium pratense*), was added to salads and soups, and a wine was made from the flowers. Medicinally, clover was taken for skin complaints, especially eczema and psoriasis; clover tea was said to stimulate liver and gall-bladder activity, improve the appetite and cure indigestion. Externally the herb was applied as a poultice to relieve inflammations, ease rheumatic aches and pains. Culpeper said that made into an ointment the herb '*is good to apply to the bites of venomous creatures*'.

The beautiful **dog roses** or **briars** (*rosa canna*) cannot be missed in the hedgerows during June and the hips, gathered in December are rich in vitamin C. The leaves were used as a mild laxative and, being astringent, for healing wounds. Rose water made a soothing antiseptic tonic for sore and sensitive skins.

Eglantine or **sweetbriar** (*rosa rubiginosa*) grows wild in woodland and on the edges of fields. The seed oil was applied externally to help regenerate skin and scar tissue, and to heal burns and scalds. Culpeper said that the hips of the eglantine: '*If made into a conserve, and eaten occasionally, gently bind the belly, stop defluxions of the head and stomach, help digestion, sharpen the appetite, and dry up the moisture of cold rheum and phlegm upon the stomach.*'

Foxglove (*digitalis purpurea*) according to Culpeper, was '*used by the Italians to heal fresh wounds, the leaves being bound thereon. The juice is used to cleanse, dry and heal old sores. The decoction with some sugar or honey cleanses and purges the body.*' Modern herbalists do not use foxglove because of its cumulative toxic effects.

Honeysuckle or **woodbine** (*lonicera periclymenum*) berries are extremely poisonous, nevertheless the plant was used for treating colds, asthma, constipation, skin infections and urinary complains. Gerard said that: '*The flowers steeped in oil, and set in* *the sun, are good to anoint the body that is benumbed, and grown very cold.'* Fresh flowers were added to salads, or made into a substitute tea.

Monkshood or **wolf's bane** (*aconitum napellus*) is extremely poisonous, but still used in various medical preparations as a pain-killer and sedative. Pliny said that: *'It is in its nature to kill a human being unless in that being it finds something else to destroy.'* Gerard warned against trusting the appearance of a plant that *'beareth very gair and goodly blue flowers in shape like a helmet; which are so beautiful that a man would think they were of some excellent virtue'.*

Deadly nightshade (*atropa belladonna*), **enchanter's nightshade** (*circaea lutetiana*) and **woody nightshade** or **bittersweet** (*solanum dulcamara*) can be seen this month. Deadly nightshade lives up to its reputation although it has many uses in modern medicine. Before the advent of modern anaesthetics it was applied to the skin as 'sorcerer's pomade' to make the patient unconscious before surgery. Excess use causes respiratory failure and death and should not be used in any herbal treatments. Enchanter's nightshade is actually a member of the willow herb family and is no relation to its deadly and woody namesakes; it has been used to treat wounds, but there is no useful or medical properties recorded for the plant. Woody nightshade is an astringent, cooling herb with a bitter then sweet taste. It lowers fever and has diuretic, expectorant, sedative and anti-rheumatic effects; should only be used by qualified practitioners as use can paralyse the central nervous system. Culpeper said: *'It is good to remove witchcraft both in men and beast, and all sudden diseases whatsoever. Country people bruised the berries and applied them to felons, thereby ridding their fingers of such troublesome guests.'*

Field poppy (*papaver rhoes*) can be used to prepare a syrup from the seeds and flowers in the treatment of coughs, throat infections, chest complaints, insomnia and whooping cough. Externally the plant was used to cool inflammation, ease pains and relieve migraine. Ripe poppy seeds were sprinkled on bread and cakes; oil from the seeds was also used in cooking and the flowers were used to colour wine.

Yellow iris (*iris pseudacorus*) or **flag** is found in marshes, wet woods and wet ground by rivers, lakes and ditches. An infusion of the dried root has been used to check diarrhoea and leucor-rhoea, and to ease menstrual pains. The sap of the plant is purgative and emetic and very bitter; it is toxic in large doses and can cause blisters if applied to the skin.

July

This month often provides a breathing space before the manic weeks of the harvest and this is the time for the agricultural shows to take place all over the country. In every valley pale shimmering fields of freshly-mown hay make a mosaic against the grain fields, which now mellow to the bronze of the harvest.

Out in the cornfields the brilliant blue petals of the **cornflower** (*centaurea cyanus*) were picked to use fresh in salads, while an infusion of the juices was prescribed for digestive and gastric disorders. The flowers were also used to produce a lotion for sore and tired eyes. Culpeper said that: *'The juice put into fresh or green wounds doth quickly solder up the lips of them together, and is very effectual to heal all ulcers and sores in the mouth.'* The petals were also used to colour ink, cosmetics and medicines.

Ox-eye daisy (*leucanthemum vulgare*) is similar in action to chamomile, which is the more popular herb; it has diuretic, anti-spasmodic and tonic properties, but is emetic if more than the recommended dose is taken. Culpeper said: *'The leaves bruised and applied to the testicles or any other part that is swollen and hot, doth dissolve it and temper the heat.'*

On the banks of the stream **purple loosestrife** (*lythrurn salicaria*) can be found in variety of wetland habitats including freshwater, tidal and non-tidal marshes, river banks and ditches. Although scarcely used at present, loosestrife has been highly esteemed by many herbalists, it is well established in the treatment of chronic diarrhoea and dysentery, and is used in leucorrhoea and blood-spitting. It has also been prescribed for fevers, liver diseases, constipation and for outward application to wounds and sores. A warm gargle and drink has been used to treat quinsy or a scrofulous throat.

August

This month is the thrilling climax to the farming year with all the excitement and satisfaction of harvest time. In these silent days of late summer, the first flickering tints of autumn begin to show, while warming winds rustle the ripening ears of corn, bending the grain like the roll of the sea, or the sigh of some distant tide.

There are two sorts of **bilberry** (*vaccinium myrtillu*) or **wortle-berries** – the red and the black – that can be found in forests and on heathland. When used medicinally, the berries act as an astringent diuretic; the dried berries administered in the form of decoction are effective for diarrhoea and dysentery. Culpeper observed: *'It is a pity they are used no more in physic than they are.'*

Fig-wort (*scrophularia nodosa*). Medieval herbalists used figwort to treat 'king's evil', or scrofula, a tubercular disease of the lymph glands in the neck. Despite its unpleasant smell, it was also used as a mild laxative, a heart stimulant, a pain reliever and a blood cleansing tonic. Applied externally, figwort was used for sores, scratches, minor wounds and skin diseases. As Culpeper said: *'A better remedy cannot be for the king's evil, because the Moon that rules the disease is exalted there.'*

Heather (*calluna vulgaris*) or **ling** is native to Britain, growing on moors and heathland. 'Ling' is derived from the Old English for fire, and refers to the plant's importance as a fuel in Anglo-Saxon times, as well as for thatching and bedding. Medicinally, preparations of heather were prescribed for urinary and kidney problems. It was also used to relieve rheumatic and arthritic pains, and as a mild sedative.

The roots of **harebells** (*campanula rotundifolia*), also known as Scottish bluebells, were applied as a compress to heal wounds, stanch bleeding and reduce inflammation. In folklore it was believed to belong to the Devil and was associated with witches, the Faere Folk and other supernatural beings.

Field scabious (*knautia arvensis*) of which Culpeper said: '*It is effective for all sorts of coughs, shortness of breath, and all other diseases of the chest and lungs,*' and **Lesser Field Scabious** (*scabiosa columbaria*) have similar medicinal virtues. Culpeper commented about the latter: '*The herb bruised and applied, in a short time loosens and draws out any splinter, or broken bone lying in the flesh.*' The plant is not popular with modern herbalists. **Devil's bit scabious** (*succisa pratensis*) is abundant in marshes, pastures, and hedgerows, but as Culpeper observed: '*This used to be an important medicinal herb, but that is no longer the case.*' However, it was said to put a stop to any evil directed toward you.

Going back to the Middle Ages, **St John's wort** (*hypericum perforatum*) was used for nervous exhaustion, epilepsy, depression, insomnia, bronchial catarrh, stomach complaints and madness. Externally, it was used for wounds (particularly deep sword cuts) sores, burns, bruises, inflammations, sprains, haemorrhoids and nerve pains, such as neuralgia and sciatica. The fresh leaves were added to salads.

White water lilies (*nymphaea alba*) are found in pools, standing water and slow-running streams and rivers, and the root is used as an an-aphrodisiac to reduce sexual excitement. It is also prescribed for a wide variety of skin complaints. Culpeper said: '*It settles the brain of frantic persons.*' Conversely, in homeopathic medicine the **yellow pond lily** (*nuphar lutea*) is prescribed to increase the sperm count and increase sexual desire; it has also been used in the treatment of syphilis and skin dermatitis.

September

Now the fields are green and gold – green where the roots crops are still growing and golden where the stubble left after the corn harvest awaits the plough. Mists linger in the valley, rolling across the newly-ploughed earth which now breaks the harvest stubble. Swallows gather together in flocks over the empty fields, their leaving generally coinciding with Michaelmas Day – 29th September – a date which traditionally marks the end of harvesting.

Marsh mallow (*althaea officinalis*) was said by Pliny that *'whoever swallows half a cyathus [wine ladle] of the juice a day shall be immune to all diseases.'* In England fresh mallow leaves were used as a poultice for wounds, bruises, sprains, inflammations, stings and insect bites. They were also used to treat coughs, chest and lung complaints, diarrhoea, insomnia, cystitis and gastric ulcers. Listed by Aelfric, mallow leaves were also eaten as a vegetable and added to salads, soups and stews. The modern sugary confectionary known as marshmallow, which contains no herbal extracts, originated from a soothing sweet recipe made from the powdered root of the plant.

Great mullein or **Aaron's rod** (*verbascum thapsus*) is potentially poisonous, but was prescribed in the Middle Ages for coughs, respiratory disorders, and all inflammatory ailments. Externally, it was used to treat burns, wounds, ulcers and skin diseases. The smoke from the burning leaves was inhaled to relieve asthma. Its country name, 'hag's taper' refers to the plant's use in rites, potions and spells of witches.

The astringent juice of **ragwort** (*senecio jacobaea*) was used for wounds, ulcers, sores, burns and inflammations. Its country name 'cankerwort' refers to its use in the treatment of cancerous ulcers. As a poultice the herb was used for aching joints, swellings, rheumatic pains, sciatica and gout: Culpeper said: *'The decoction of the herb is good to wash the mouth or throat that has ulcers or sores therein'*. Another country name, 'staggerwort' arose from the mistaken belief that the plant had the power to cure horses of staggers, a disease of the brain and spinal cord. The plant can be harmful to cattle, even if included among the dry hay crop.

Toad-flax (*linaria vulgaris*) was prescribed for constipation, dropsy, kidney complaints, liver diseases, scrofula, enteritis, hepatitis and gall bladder problems. Externally the herb was used for cuts, haemorrhoids, sores, malignant ulcers, skin rashes and conjunctivitis. The herb should not be taken during pregnancy and during the Middle Ages it was used for laundry starch and boiled in milk as a fly poison.

Needless to say, not all wild flowers with medicinal properties have been included, but following on from The Wildlife and Countryside Act of 1981 it is now illegal to pick some wild flowers in Great Britain. Generally, uprooting is considered harmful, but picking with care and in moderation usually does little damage. However, in some cases picking can be harmful and may even be illegal.

Warning: Anyone seriously interested in wort-lore should first obtain a copy of *RHS Encyclopaedia of Herbs and Their Uses* by Deni Brown, which gives the historical, traditional and modern pharmaceutical uses for more than 1,000 plants. Some plants in common use in the past have been discovered by medical research to be highly dangerous if wrongly administered by a well-meaning amateur herbalist.

Country Crafts

In the pursuit of country crafts it is possible to forge another link with the past, and the traditional broom represents this ancient heritage whether it is used in the home or in the garden. Country people produced baskets to contain their household goods and chattels and there is a certain satisfaction in cutting the wood to make household items for gifts or personal use.

Birch and Heath Brooms

There is a knack to making a broom or besom, and this description was taken from Gertrude Jekyll's *Old West Surrey* published before 1923 that describes the process:

> The birch spray is not used fresh. It is put aside to dry and toughen for some months. Then they 'break birch for brooms'. A faggot is opened, and the spray is broken by hand to the right size and laid in bundles. Breaking birch is often women's work. The 'bonds' that fasten the spray on to the handle are of hazel or withy [willow], split and shaved with the knife into thick ribbons. They are soaked in water to make them lissom.
>
> The broom-squarer gathers up the spray round the end of the [hazel] stick, sitting in front of a heavy fixed block to which the further end of a bond is made fast. He pushes the near end of the bond into the butts of the spray, nearly at a right angle to the binding. He then binds by rolling the broom away from him, pulling it tight as it goes. When he had wound up to the length of the bond, the end is released and pushed into the work. Heath [heather] brooms have two bonds; birch, which are made much longer, have three. A hole is bored between the strands of spray and through the stick, and a peg driven tightly through, so that the spray cannot slip off the stick. The rough butts are then trimmed off, and the broom is complete.

The birch is known as the 'Lady of the Woods' and the actual brush part of the witch's traditional besom is symbolic of the female component, which is made up of birch twigs. The handle is the male component, often with a phallic shaping to the top and fashioned from alder or ash. Because the besom was an important implement in witchcraft it was believed that to identify a witch all that was needed was to place the broom across the threshold at an awkward angle so that the witch would be obliged to take it up because she could not step over it. It was also said that an unmarried woman stepping over a broom would bear a bastard child.

Thumb Sticks and Staffs

Making a thumb stick or staff is a long process and almost any wood can be used, with ash or hazel being the most traditional for magical working; and the first step is to find a natural branch of suitable length and thickness. The thumb stick should be held with the thumb in the V at chest height to provide a comfortable and safe grip; while the staff should be almost as tall as its user.

Staffs were often used for divining direction and the traditional way of deciding which way to go was to stand the staff upright and let it fall where it will. In *Root & Branch: British Magical Tree Lore* the symbolism of the different woods chosen for a staff revealed that these were always subtly set apart from the traditional hazel stick carried by countrymen. The length of the thumb stick if being used for magical purposes should be cut so that the V for the thumb is exactly at eye level of the person using it.

Basketry

There are many different kinds of baskets – hard baskets, soft baskets, baskets of rush, reed, sedge, and baskets of straw – and each has a different method of cutting, storing and treatment of the materials. For hard basketry the most popular are hazel, willow and dogwood for weaving and dogwood, lime, and willow for the stakes. The wood should be cut in the autumn and stored in the dark. For soft basketry use rushes and reeds that should have been cut around Midsummer Day. Cut as near the roots as possible, dry them in the shade and store them in a cool, dark outhouse. Sedges should be cut in August, tied in bundles and dried in the sun, before storing in a dry shed. Good quality wheat straw can be used for making light baskets suitable for gift-giving.

Hurdle Making

This is a country craft that dates back to when shepherds ceased to be itinerant workers. In northern parts of the country the hill shepherd constructed permanent and solid folds for the sheep from the stones that littered the landscape; on the rolling downlands in the south there is no stone, but there was a wealth of hazel that grew in abundance in the woodlands and the trade of the hurdle-maker was born. The moveable pen was light, roughly three feet in height and six feet long and, in order to keep them upright, the framework incorporated holes into which pointed poles were inserted and driven into the ground. The hurdles were made where the coppice wood grew and, since only mature hazel would serve the purpose, there needed to be a good supply. The hurdle maker still finds an outlet for his skill and hurdles can often be bought (or sold) at local garden centres.

Footnote: What Am I?

The Secret People is a wander down memory lane and a step back in time; it is that 'other country' of the past where parish-pump witches, wise women and cunning folk still travel the highways and byways of a bygone era. Their voices can still be heard in the recipes and remedies handed down via an oral tradition, and now giving new knowledge to the next generation of pagans. It was a world where men went out with a ferret in a box and a long-net, accompanied by a silent long dog for a companion under a 'poacher's moon'.

From 'owl-light' until dawn these people walked silently in the woods and along the hedgerows, watching and waiting to collect Nature's bounty to be used for the benefit of themselves and their neighbours. From them came the introduction to spells and charms, divination and fortune-telling; the language of birds and the movement of animals – all grist for the witch's mill. Mysterious horsemen might share secrets of horseshoe nails and thunder-water; while countrymen lived by weather, the seedtime and the harvest.

Few of *The Secret People* could be called traditional witches by any stretch of the imagination, and many would have been mortally offended to be referred to as a 'witch' or 'pagan'. Few parish-pump witches would have thought about the skills they possessed since these were natural abilities, and even fewer wise women and cunning folk would have had any concept of the sombre and often dangerous rituals required for the raising of energy needed in the practice of true witchcraft. Theirs was a knowledge that filtered down in the form of spells, domestic plant medicine and country lore, imparted to offspring, friends and neighbours, who in turn handed it down to their children...and so on down through the generations. In fact, in his *Dialogue Concerning Witches & Witchcraft* (1603) George Gifford observed that local wise women 'doth more good in one year than all these scripture men will do so long as they live'.

Most, however, would live by the Church calendar, inveigling saints to add potency to their healing spells, or to guide a hand in locating missing property; with many of the protective charms being aimed at deflecting malevolent witchcraft! Most old ladies in the parish seemed to have a wide repertoire of fortune-telling tricks to amuse young girls looking for a husband, not to mention the applied psychology of already knowing their neighbours' business, which made divination with playing cards and tea-leaves a push-over, and even up until recent years the village fete always had a fortune-telling tent. And since the early Church calendar had been formed around the agricultural year, the men folk of the village had no problem with presenting themselves, their animals, and produce from the harvest for blessing.

The Secret People would have greatly outnumbered the practitioners of traditional witchcraft since the practical abilities that define a true witch are bred in the bone and not everyone can lay claim to the lineage. The skills of *The Secret People* can, however, be learned and perfected with practise and for those who struggle to find a label with which to empathise, it is hoped the lessons taught here will help the reader to establish some sort of identity that sits comfortably with them.

Today, under the ubiquitous umbrella of paganism, the parish-pump witch runs the occult shop in the high street, the wise woman dispenses Reiki healing and the cunning man has become a professional tarot reader. The countryman's world has disappeared under a sprawl of urban housing and ring roads, while the poacher has yielded his domain to the brutal gangs who slaughter wildlife on a commercial scale – even the poacher's dog, the lurcher, has found his niche in the 'fly-ball' event at Crufts!

And yet...the knowledge of *The Secret People* is still there for the learning, if only we know how to search for it and rediscover our identity.

Sources and Bibliography

Akenfield, Ronald Blythe, (Penguin)

The Book of Divining the Future, Eva Shaw (Wordsworth)

Brother Cadfael's Herb Garden: Medieval Plants & Their Uses, Rob Talbot and Robin Whiteman (Little Brown)

The Complete Herbal, Nicholas Culpeper (Wordsworth)

The Confessions of a Poacher (1890), Anon (Old House Books)

Country Book, Malcolm Saville (Cassel)

The Countryman's Weekend Book, Eric Parker (Seeley)

Country Seasons, Philip Clucas (Windward)

The Countryside Cookbook, Gail Duff (Prism Press)

Culpeper's Colour Herbal, Ed. David Potterton (Foulsham)

Culpeper's Complete Herbal, (Wordsworth.

Culpeper's Medicine, Graeme Tobyn (Element)

English Country Traditions, Ian Niall (Running Press)

Food For Free, Richard Mabey (Collins Gem)

Granny's Natural Remedies, Brenda Evans (Canary Press)

Green Magic, Lesley Gordon (Webb & Bower)

Green Pharmacy: A History of Herbal Medicine, Barbara Griggs (Norman & Hobhouse)

Healing Power of Celtic Plants, Dr Angela Paine, (Moon Books)

Herbal Simples Approved for Modern Uses of Cure, William Thomas Fernie (publisher unknown)

Herbs: Magical, Medicinal, Marvellous, Deborah J Martin (Moon Books)

A History of Food, Maguelonne Toussaint-Samat (Wiley-Blackwell)

A Kitchen Witch's World of Magical Plants and Herbs, Rachel Patterson (Moon Books)

Larousse Gastronomique, Prosper Montagne (Hamlyn English edition)

Memory, Wisdom & Healing: The History of Domestic Plant Medicine Gabrielle Hatfield (Sutton)

Mrs Beeton's Cookery Book, revised edition 1933 (Ward Lock)

The New Poacher's Handbook, Ian Niall (Country Library)
Pagan Portals: Candle Magic, Lucya Starza (Moon Books)
The Penguin Guide to the Superstitions of Britain and Ireland, Steve Roud (Penguin)
Perfume Power, Joules Taylor (London House)
The Physicians of Myddfai, Ithel
Religion and the Decline of Magic, Keith Thomas (Weidenfeld & Nicholson)
Roman Book of Days, Pauline Erina (ignotus)
Root & Branch: British Magical Tree Lore, Melusine Draco & Paul Harriss (ignotus)
RHS Encyclopaedia of Herbs and Their Uses, Deni Brown (Dorling Kindersley)
The Secret People, E W Martin (Country Book Club)
Shaman Pathways: Aubry's Dog, Melusine Draco (Moon Books)
Shaman Pathways: Black Horse, White Horse, Melusine Draco (Moon Books)
Vinegar: Nature's Secret Weapon, Maxwell Stein (Blakefield)
Weatherwise, Paul John Goldsack (David & Charles)
Witches & Neighbours, Robin Briggs (Harper Collins)
A Witch's Treasure for Hearth & Garden, Gabrielle Sidonie (ignotus)
The Woman's Treasury for Home and Garden

The following Moon Books are more specialised approaches to many of the subjects included in the text and are recommended as further reading:

Healing Power of Celtic Plants, Dr Angela Paine
Herbs: Medical, Magical, Marvellous! Deborah Marton
A Kitchen Witch's World of Magical Plants and Herbs, Rachel Patterson
A Kitchen Witch's World of Magical Food, Rachel Patterson
Pagan Portals: Candle Magic, Lucya Starza
Pagan Portals: Runes, Kylie Holmes

MOON

BOOKS

Moon Books invites you to begin or deepen your encounter with Paganism, in all its rich, creative, flourishing forms.

If you have enjoyed this book, why not tell other readers by posting a review on your preferred booksite. Recent bestsellers from Moon Books are:

Journey to the Dark Goddess
How to Return to Your Soul
Jane Meredith
Discover the powerful secrets of the Dark Goddess and transform your depression, grief and pain into healing and integration.
Paperback: 978-1-84694-677-6
ebook: 978-1-78099-223-5

Shamanic Reiki
Expanded Ways of Working with Universal Life Force Energy
Llyn Roberts, Robert Levy
Shamanism and Reiki are each powerful ways of healing; together, their power multiplies. *Shamanic Reiki* introduces techniques to help healers and Reiki practitioners tap ancient healing wisdom.
Paperback: 978-1-84694-037-8
ebook: 978-1-84694-650-9

Pagan Portals – The Awen Alone
Walking the Path of the Solitary Druid
Joanna van der Hoeven
An introductory guide for the solitary Druid, *The Awen Alone* will accompany you as you explore and seek out your own place within the natural world.
Paperback: 978-1-78279-547-6
ebook: 978-1-78279-546-9

A Kitchen Witch's World of Magical Herbs & Plants

Rachel Patterson

A journey into the magical world of herbs and plants, filled with magical uses, folklore, history and practical magic. By popular writer, blogger and kitchen witch, Tansy Firedragon.

Paperback: 978-1-78279-621-3

ebook: 978-1-78279-620-6

Medicine for the Soul

The Complete Book of Shamanic Healing

Ross Heaven

All you will ever need to know about shamanic healing and how to become your own shaman...

Paperback: 978-1-78099-419-2

ebook: 978-1-78099-420-8

Shaman Pathways – The Druid Shaman

Exploring the Celtic Otherworld

Danu Forest

A practical guide to Celtic shamanism with exercises and techniques as well as traditional lore for exploring the Celtic Otherworld.

Paperback: 978-1-78099-615-8

ebook: 978-1-78099-616-5

Find more titles and sign up to our readers' newsletter at http://www.johnhuntpublishing.com/paganism. Follow us on Facebook at https://www.facebook.com/MoonBooks and Twitter at https://twitter.com/MoonBooksJHP. Most titles are published in paperback and as an ebook. Paperbacks are available in physical bookshops. Both print and ebook editions are available online. Readers of ebooks can click on the live links in the titles to order.